OVERLEAF:

*A caravan of Semitic traders of the patriarchal period,
painted by an Egyptian artist for a tomb at Beni-hasan
c. 1900 B.C. The figure leading the procession (just after the
two Egyptian officials pictured at the extreme right)
wears a "coat of many colors," as does Joseph in the Book
of Genesis.*

THE
GIFTS
OF THE
JEWS

BY *Thomas Cahill*

THE HINGES OF HISTORY

Volume I: How the Irish Saved Civilization

Volume II: The Gifts of the Jews

Five additional volumes are planned.

THE HINGES OF HISTORY

We normally think of history as one catastrophe after
another, war followed by war, outrage by outrage—almost as if history were nothing more than all the narratives of human pain, assembled in sequence. And surely
this is, often enough, an adequate description. But history
is also the narratives of grace, the recountings of those
blessed and inexplicable moments when someone did
something for someone else, saved a life, bestowed a gift,
gave something beyond what was required by circum-
stance.

In this series, THE HINGES OF HISTORY, I mean to retell
the story of the Western world as the story of the great
gift-givers, those who entrusted to our keeping one or
another of the singular treasures that make up the patrimony of the West. This is also the story of the evolution
of Western sensibility, a narration of how we became the
people that we are and why we think and feel the way we
do. And it is, finally, a recounting of those essential moments when everything was at stake, when the mighty
stream that became Western history was in ultimate danger and might have divided into a hundred useless tribu-
taries or frozen in death or evaporated altogether. But the
great gift-givers, arriving in the moment of crisis, provided for transition, for transformation, and even for
transfiguration, leaving us a world more varied and complex, more awesome and delightful, more beautiful and
strong than the one they had found.

—THOMAS CAHILL

THE
GIFTS OF
THE JEWS

How a Tribe of Desert Nomads

Changed the Way Everyone

Thinks and Feels

✹

THOMAS CAHILL

Nan A. Talese/Anchor Books
Doubleday
New York   London   Toronto   Sydney   Auckland

PUBLISHED BY NAN A. TALESE/
ANCHOR BOOKS
imprints of Doubleday
a division of Random House, Inc.
1540 Broadway, New York, New York 10036

ANCHOR BOOKS *and* DOUBLEDAY *are*
trademarks of Doubleday,
a division of Random House, Inc.

Page 276 constitutes an extension of this copyright page.

Book design by Marysarah Quinn
Maps by Jackie Aher

The Library of Congress has cataloged the hardcover
edition of this book as follows:
Cahill, Thomas.
The Gifts of the Jews: how a tribe of desert nomads changed the
way everyone thinks and feels / Thomas Cahill.
p. cm. — (The hinges of history : vol. 2)
Includes bibliographical references and index.
1. Judaism—History—To 70 A.D. 2. Jews—History—To
70 A.D. 3. Bible. O.T.—History of Biblical events.
4. Civilization—Jewish influences. I. Title. II. Series:
Cahill, Thomas. Hinges of history : vol. 2.
BM165.C25 1998
909'.04924—DC21 97-45139
CIP

ISBN 0-385-48249-3
Copyright © 1998 by Thomas Cahill
All Rights Reserved
Printed in the United States of America
First Nan A. Talese/Anchor Books
Paperback Edition: September 1999

5 7 9 10 8 6

TO KRISTIN

How but in custom and in ceremony
Are innocence and beauty born?
Ceremony's a name for the rich horn,
And custom for the spreading laurel tree.

Everything an Indian does is in a circle, and that is because the power of the world always works in circles, and everything tries to be round. In the old days when we were a strong and happy people, all our power came to us from the sacred hoop of the nation. . . . Even the seasons form a great circle in their changing, and always come back again to where they were. The life of a man is a circle from childhood to childhood and so it is in everything where power moves.

—BLACK ELK

Unless there is
a new mind there cannot be a new
line, the old will go on
repeating itself with recurring
deadliness: without invention
nothing lies under the witch-hazel
bush.

—WILLIAM CARLOS WILLIAMS

CONTENTS

INTRODUCTION

*

The Jews Are It

The Jews started it all—and by "it" I mean so many of the things we care about, the underlying values that make all of us, Jew and gentile, believer and atheist, tick. Without the Jews, we would see the world through different eyes, hear with different ears, even feel with different feelings. And not only would our sensorium, the screen through which we receive the world, be different: we would think with a different mind, interpret all our experience differently, draw different conclusions from the things that befall us. And we would set a different course for our lives.

By "we" I mean the usual "we" of late-twentieth-century writing: the people of the Western world, whose peculiar but vital mentality has come to infect every culture on earth, so that, in a startlingly precise sense, all humanity is now willy-nilly caught up in this "we." For better or worse, the role of the West in humanity's history is singular. Because of this, the role of the Jews, the inventors of Western culture, is also singular: there is simply no one else remotely like them; theirs is a unique vocation. Indeed, as we shall see, the very idea of *vocation,* of a personal destiny, is a Jewish idea.

Our history is replete with examples of those who have refused to see what the Jews are really about, who—through intellectual blindness, racial chauvinism, xenophobia, or just plain evil—have been unable to give this oddball tribe, this raggle-taggle band, this race of wanderers who are the progenitors of the Western world, their due. Indeed, at the end of this bloodiest of centuries, we can all too easily look back on scenes of unthinkable horror perpetrated by those who would do anything rather than give the Jews their due.

But I must ask my readers to erase from their minds not only the horrors of history—modern, medieval, and ancient—but (so far as one can) the very notion of history itself. More especially, we must erase from our minds all the suppositions on which our world is built—the whole intricate edifice of actions and ideas that are our intellectual and emotional patrimony. We must reimagine ourselves in the form of humanity that lived and moved on this planet before the first word of the Bible was written down, before it was spoken, before it was even dreamed.

What a bizarre phenomenon the first human mutants must have appeared upon the earth. Like their primate progenitors, they were long-limbed and rangy, but, with unimpressive muscles and without significant fur or claws, confined to the protection of trees, save when they would tentatively essay the floor of the savannah—hoping to obtain food without becoming food. With their small mouths and underdeveloped teeth, their unnaturally large heads (like the heads of primate infants), they were forced back on their wits. Their young remained helpless for years, well past the infancy of other mammals, requiring from their parents long years of vigilance and extensive tutelage in many things. Without planning and forethought, without in fact the development of complex strategies, these mutants could not hope to survive at all.

But if we make use of what hints remain in the prehistorical and protohistorical "record," we must còme to the unexpected conclusion that their inventions and discoveries, made in aid of their survival and prosperity—tools and fire, then agriculture and beasts of burden, then irrigation and the wheel—did not seem to them innovations. These were gifts from beyond the world, somehow part of the Eternal. All evidence points to there having been, in the earliest religious thought, a vision of the cosmos that was profoundly cyclical. The assumptions that early man made about the world were, in all their essentials, little different from the assumptions that later and more sophisticated societies, like Greece and India, would make in a more elaborate manner. As Henri-Charles Puech says of Greek thought in his seminal *Man and Time:* "No event is unique, nothing is enacted but once . . . ; every event has been enacted, is enacted, and will be enacted perpetually; the same individuals have appeared, appear, and will appear at every turn of the circle."

The Jews were the first people to break out of this circle, to find a new way of thinking and experiencing, a new way of understanding and feeling the world, so much so that it may be said with some justice that theirs is the only new idea that human beings have ever had. But their worldview has become so much a part of us that at this point it might as well have been written into our cells as a genetic code. We find it so impossible to shed—even for a brief experiment—that it is now the cosmic vision of all *other* peoples that appears to us exotic and strange.

The Bible is the record *par excellence* of the Jewish religious experience, an experience that remains fresh and even shocking when it is read against the myths of other ancient literatures. The word *bible* comes from the Greek plural form *biblia,* meaning "books." And though the Bible is rightly considered *the* book of the Western world—its foundation document—it is actually a collection of books, a various library written almost entirely in Hebrew over the course of a thousand years.

We have scant evidence concerning the early development of Hebrew, one of a score of Semitic tongues that arose in the Middle East during a period that began sometime before the start of the second millennium B.C.*—how long before we do not know. Some of these tongues, such as Akkadian, found literary expression fairly early, but there is no reliable record of written Hebrew before the tenth century B.C.—that is, till well after the resettlement of the Israelites in Canaan following their escape from Egypt under the leadership of Moses, the greatest of all proto-Jewish figures. This means that the supposedly historical stories of at least the first books of the Bible were preserved originally not as written texts but as

* Recently, the designations B.C.E. (before the common era) and C.E. (common era), used originally in Jewish circles to avoid the Christian references contained in the designations B.C. (before Christ) and A.D. *(anno domini,* in the year of the Lord), have gained somewhat wider currency. I use B.C. and A.D. not to cause offense to anyone but because the new designations, still largely unrecognized outside scholarly circles, can unnecessarily disorient the common reader.

oral tradition. So, from the wanderings of Abraham in Canaan through the liberation from Egypt wrought by Moses to the Israelite resettlement of Canaan under Joshua, what we are reading are oral tales, collected and edited for the first (but not the last) time in the tenth century during and after the kingship of David. But the full collection of texts that make up the Bible (short of the Greek New Testament, which would not be appended till the first century of our era) did not exist in its current form till well after the Babylonian Captivity of the Jews—that is, till sometime after 538 B.C. The last books to be taken into the canon of the Hebrew Bible probably belong to the third and second centuries B.C., these being Esther and Ecclesiastes (third century) and Daniel (second century). Some apocryphal books, such as Judith and the Wisdom of Solomon, are as late as the first century.

To most readers today, the Bible is a confusing hodgepodge; and those who take up the daunting task of reading it from cover to cover seldom maintain their resolve beyond a book or two. Though the Bible is full of literature's two great themes, love and death (as well as its exciting caricatures, sex and violence), it is also full of tedious ritual prescriptions and interminable battles. More than anything, because the Bible is the product of so many hands over so many ages, it is full of confusion for the modern reader who attempts to decode what it might be about.

But to understand ourselves—and the identity we carry so effortlessly that most "moderns" no longer give any thought to the origins of attitudes we have come to take as natural and self-evident—we must return to this great document, the cornerstone of Western civilization. My purpose is not to write an introduction to the Bible, still less to Judaism, but to discover in this unique culture of the Word some essential thread that runs through it, to uncover in outline the sensibility that undergirds the whole structure, and to identify the still-living sources of our Western heritage for contemporary readers, whatever color of the belief-unbelief spectrum they may inhabit.

To appreciate the Bible properly, we cannot begin with it. All definitions must limit or set boundaries, must show what the thing-to-be-defined is not. So we begin before the Bible, before the Jews, before Abraham—in the time when reality seemed to be a great circle, closed and predictable in its revolutions. We return to the world of the Wheel.

ONE

THE TEMPLE IN THE MOONLIGHT

✳

The Primeval Religious Experience

Somewhat more than five millennia ago, a human hand first carved a written word, and so initiated history, mankind's recorded story. This happened in Sumer, probably in a warehouse of Uruk, perhaps the earliest human habitation to deserve the name of "city," massed along the Euphrates River in ancient Mesopotamia—modern Warka in present-day Iraq. The written word was an invention born of necessity: how else were the Sumerians to keep their accounts straight? The novel agglomeration of human beings and their possessions into a city such as Uruk—a mind-defeating jumble of temples, dwellings, storerooms, and alleyways, an agglomeration soon to be imitated throughout the ancient world—cried out for a new way of counting shipments and recalling transactions, for a man's memory was no longer sufficient to encompass such immensities. The human mind wearied before the task, growing resistant and uncooperative—and, at last, alarmingly error-prone—but human ingenuity proposed a damnably clever solution: enduring written symbols to replace fallible human memory.

This innovation, which would change forever the course of the human story, making possible fantastic feats of information storage and retrieval and wholly new forms of communication, both interpersonal and corporate, had been prepared for by other innovations that had preceded it over the long centuries of the Sumerians' trial-and-error ascent to urbanization. The invention of agriculture—the discovery that one need not wait upon the bounty of nature but can organize that bounty more or less predictably through the seasonal planting of seed—had greatly lessened man's reliance on the uncertain harvests of hunting and gathering and had made possible the first settled communities, organized around a dependable grain supply. The domestication of flocks and herds for predictable yields of eggs, milk, flesh, leather, and wool soon followed (or may even have occurred earlier). The invention of the hoe and the further invention of the plow—which probably occurred when some lazy but sly farmer thought to tie his hoe to a rope hitched to the horn of an ox, thus giving himself considerably more muscle power through the ox's strength and enabling him to farm a far larger territory—went a long way toward creating stable farming communities throughout the Fertile Crescent, that great arch of watered land stretching north from the Tigris-Euphrates plain, turning south through the Jordan valley, and ending at the Sinai. Someone's brilliant idea to dig trenches (and then to fashion canals and reservoirs) so that river water could run controllably from higher embankments to lower fields meant that the farmer no longer had to wait for the uncertain rains of the Middle East but could now farm fields he would once have looked on as useless. This technique, refined to exquisite perfection over many centuries, would at last make possible along the broad steppes of the Tigris-Euphrates plain the Hanging Gardens of Babylon (Babylonia being the direct successor to Sumer), that stupendous wonder of the world, a detailed description of which became the favorite party piece of ancient tourists, thus enabling them to bore their friends to death long before the invention of photography.

Then, the period just before the invention of written language saw in Sumer an explosion of technological creativity on a scale that would not be matched till the nineteenth and twentieth centuries of our era. For this period witnessed not only the sudden expansion of farming communities with their growing inventory of agricultural and pastoral innovations, but wheeled transport, sailing ships, metallurgy, and wheel-turned, oven-baked pottery—all appearing, as it were, within weeks of one another. The Sumerians were the first to hit upon the methods of construction that enable human beings to go beyond the simpler feat of providing comfortable shelter for themselves and to erect vastly impressive, even overwhelming enclosures for business and ritual: monumental stone sculpture, engraving, and inlay, the brick mold, the arch, the vault, and the dome all first came to light under the dazzling Sumerian sun. Cumulatively, this unique series of creations made possible for the first time ecumenical trading and, thence, great concentrations of people and possessions and, particularly, the gigantic storage facilities that would encourage our unknown inventor to dream up writing.

By the time the first word was incised on a small clay tablet (which would for many centuries remain the common medium of record), Sumer had risen to dominate all Mesopotamia and had strong trading links and occasionally even political suzerainty as far away as the Nile valley in northern Africa and the Indus valley in the Far East. To the ever-

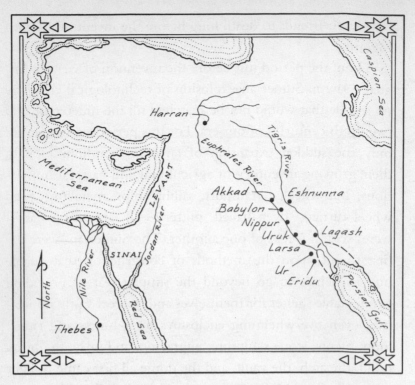

THE FERTILE CRESCENT IN THE THIRD MILLENNIUM

*This most ancient cradle of civilization was a great arc of richly irrigated land
stretching from the Persian Gulf northwest across the whole Tigris-Euphrates
plain, then southwest along the Levant–Jordan River valley and ending at the
Sinai. The principal Sumerian-Akkadian city-states are shown (including
Babylon, which belongs to a later period). The broken line indicates the shore
of the Gulf in the third millennium* B.C.

circling vultures, who no doubt took a dim view of civilization and its unfortunate paucity of easy victims, Sumer appeared a collection of some twenty-five city-states, remark-

ably uniform in culture and organization. But to the human hordes of Amorites—Semitic nomads wandering the mountains and deserts just beyond the pale of Sumer—the tiered and clustered cities, strung out along the green banks of the meandering Euphrates like a giant's necklace of polished stone, seemed shining things, each surmounted by a wondrous temple and ziggurat dedicated to the city's god-protector, each city noted for some specialty—all invidious reminders of what the nomads did not possess.

What the nomads did not possess is nicely enumerated in this Sumerian description of a typical Amorite:

> A tent-dweller buffeted by wind and rain, he knows not
>   prayers,
> With the weapon he makes the mountain his habitation,
> Contentious to excess, he turns against the land, knows not
>   to bend the knee,
> Eats uncooked meat,
> Has no house in his lifetime,
> Is not brought to burial when he dies.

This is almost a description of an animal: without manners or courtesy—even toward the dead—without religion or even cooking fire, the nomads were always getting themselves into bloody disputes with more "civilized" landowners. Behind the description we can detect the prejudice of imperialists throughout history, who blithely assume their superiority, moral as well as technical, over those whom they have marginalized and therefore their divine right to whatever is valuable, especially the land.

Thanks to the work of pioneering archaeologists, who have dug up many Sumerian cities during this century and painstakingly translated their abundant clay treasures, there is much we now know of Sumer, the world's first civilization. Sumerian techniques of farming and husbandry were extraordinarily sophisticated (the Sumerians had two hundred words just for varieties of sheep); their mathematics enabled them to do square roots and cube roots and to calculate accurately the size of a field or a building and to excavate or enlarge a canal. Their medicine was practical, not magical, and their pharmacopoeias prescribed remedies for everything from battle wounds to venereal disease (called "a disease of the *tun* and the *nu*"—and though the experts tell us they cannot be sure of the meaning of these two words, the layman will have little trouble identifying them).

We even know much about Sumerian imagination. Manuals of instruction were often written in the name of a god: a manual on farming (a perennial best-seller, since copies of it have turned up everywhere in the Sumerian ruins) claims to be authored by the god Ninurta, "trustworthy farmer of Enlil"—the great god of the Sumerian pantheon. The human farmer is advised to watch carefully over his crop and to take all precautions, both human and superhuman: "After the sprout has broken through the ground" he is to scare off the flying birds, but he is also to pray to Ninkilim, goddess of field mice, so that she will keep her sharp-toothed little subjects away from the growing grain. Even the process of brewing (the Sumerians were great beer drinkers) had a sponsoring divinity, Ninkasi, a goddess born of "sparkling-fresh water," whose name means "the lady who fills the mouth." On this subject the Sumerians would wax poetic: Ninkasi was brewer to the gods themselves, she who "bakes with lofty shovel the sprouted barley," who "mixes the *bappir*-malt with sweet aromatics," who "pours the fragrant beer in the *lahtan*-vessel which is like the Tigris and Euphrates joined!"

We mustn't take too seriously every mention of the gods in the Sumerian tablets, any more than we take seriously the pious invocation of our own God by today's public figures. The Sumerians were practical, down-to-earth businessmen, more interested in calculating the extent of their fields and the capacity of their warehouses than they were in anything else. But this does not mean that they had no worldview beyond the steady acquisition of possessions.

The worldview of a people, though normally left unspoken in the daily business of buying and selling and counting shekels, is to be found in a culture's stories, myths, and rituals, which, if studied aright, inevitably yield insight into the deepest concerns of a people by unveiling the invisible fears and desires inscribed on human hearts. The stories of Sumer, as resurrected from its plain clay tablets, possess a burnished splendor that cannot but affect contemporary readers, giving us flickering glimpses into the childhood of human imagination. Virtually all the tablets are damaged, leaving us with holes in every narrative. But many of the stories exist in several versions (so that the holes in one version can sometimes be filled in with passages from another) and even in different languages, allowing us to reconstruct, at least partially, a process of dynamic development that took place over many centuries. For the process of Sumerian storytelling itself we may be partly indebted to the wandering Semitic tribes, who, being illiterate, possessed the inexhaustible narrative memory of illiterate peoples and sometimes earned their keep by telling stories to the settled folk. These tales, whether from nomadic minstrels or from the oral traditions of the city-dwellers themselves, were eventually written down by Sumerian scribes, who did their best to categorize the wayward material into orderly groupings, thus creating "books"—in actuality, uniform series of tablets—of continuous narrative, episodic and sometimes intergenerational.

Sometimes too orderly. The Sumerian grouping of the narratives of their kings—the so-called King List—is completely useless to modern historians. These thumbnail sketches of each reign are arranged according to principles of symmetry and numerology to please the eye and ring satisfyingly on the ear, but without the least regard for what may in fact have occurred in Sumerian history. Some of the kings are said to rule for thousands of years, others for mere centuries; and recent studies, comparing these lists with other ancient records, have found that kings whose reigns are listed in sequence were actually contemporaries or near contemporaries, ruling neighboring Sumerian city-states.

The purposes of a modern historian would indeed have had no meaning in Sumer, for Sumerians—paradoxically, since they invented writing, the instrument that makes history possible—had no sense of history. The city-states had been founded by gods in time immemorial; and it was the gods who had given the Sumerians, "the black-headed people" (as they called themselves), all the tools and weapons and marvelous inventions that *we* know were the products of their own ingenuity. "Development" and "evolution"—words of such importance to us—would have meant little in the timeless culture of Sumer, where everything that was—their city, their fields, their herds, their plows—had always been.

Even their stories miss a sense of development: they begin in the middle and end in the middle. They lack the relentless necessity that we associate with storytelling, from which we demand a beginning, a middle, an end: a shape. When reading a book or watching a movie that seems to wander without direction, we ask impatiently, "Where is this going?" But all Sumerian stories are shaggy-dog stories, sounding sometimes like the patter of small children who imitate the jokes they have heard from older children without realizing that there has to be a punchline. When perusing Sumerian literature, the modern reader is often left waiting for the punchline. Despite this, the tales of ancient Sumer are full of pleasure for us, both because of their archaic strangeness and because of the occasional mirror-moments in which we are startled to glimpse something of ourselves: an image or emotion that we have in common with this people of the dim past.

———

The Sumerian work that has left the greatest impress on contemporary imagination is the *Epic of Gilgamesh,* the story of a legendary hero who probably flourished toward the middle of the third millennium B.C. as king of Uruk, the very city where writing was likely invented. He may have been of Semitic, rather than Sumerian, stock because, at least according to one translation of the notoriously unreliable King List, Lugalbanda, Gilgamesh's father and king before him, "was a nomad." If so, the nomadic minstrels would have had much reason to celebrate his exploits; and Gilgamesh's kingship would represent an early power grab by the wandering Semitic tribes, who by millennium's end would wrest power throughout Sumer and establish their languages at the expense of Sumerian. Sumerian, a language for which no cognate tongues have been found, was replaced early in the second millennium by Akkadian (or Old Babylonian) as the *lingua franca* of Mesopotamia, after which Sumerian lived on only as a literary language employed by learned scribes for special documents. But the new Semitic rulers took up not only cuneiform writing but the mythology and beliefs of their Sumerian predecessors in seamless continuity, which is why we have found stories of Gilgamesh not only in Sumerian but in Akkadian and other ancient languages.

The *Epic* opens on a charming description of ancient Uruk, with the poet acting as tour guide to a first-time visitor:

> See its wall, which is like a copper band,
> Survey its battlements, which nobody else can match,

Take the threshold, which is from time immemorial,
Approach Eanna, the home of Ishtar,*
Which no future king nor any man will ever match!
Go up on the wall of Uruk and walk around!
Inspect the foundation platform and scrutinize the
    brickwork!
Testify that its bricks are baked bricks,
That the Seven Counselors must have laid its foundations!
One square mile is city, one square mile is orchards, one
    square mile is claypits, as well as the open ground of
    Ishtar's temple.
Three square miles and the open ground comprise Uruk.

The poet's pride in the splendor and extent of his city is
unmistakable. Uruk is "from time immemorial," its foundations laid by the Seven Counselors, the gods who brought
the black-heads all the special skills and crafts that have made
them great. True greatness belongs exclusively to this
"time immemorial," and "no fu-
ture king nor any man will ever
match" such primeval achieve-
ments as the Eanna, Uruk's temple to Ishtar, goddess of love and
war. Then, as if he were working
from a shooting script for a
movie, the poet, having given us
his establishing shots of the ancient city, invites us to have a
closer look at one of the wonders

> * The great goddess of Uruk is
> named Ishtar in Akkadian (or Old
> Babylonian), the Semitic language of
> the text on which this translation is
> based, but in earlier records—in the
> Sumerian language—she is called
> Innana. This change in the names of
> the gods from Sumerian to
> Akkadian is not unlike the change
> that occurs in the transition from
> the Greek pantheon to the Roman:
> from Zeus to Jupiter, from
> Aphrodite to Venus. Throughout
> this chapter the gods are invoked by
> their Akkadian names.

it contains, a secret document preserved on a slab of Sumer's most precious material:

> Look for the copper tablet-box,
> Undo its bronze lock,
> Open the door to its secret,
> Lift out the lapis lazuli tablet, read it,
> The story of that man, Gilgamesh, who went through all
>   kinds of sufferings.
> He was superior to other kings, a warrior lord of great
>   stature,
> A hero born of Uruk, a goring wild bull.
> He marches at the front as leader,
> He goes behind, the support of his brothers,
> A strong net, the protection of his men,
> The raging flood-wave, which can destroy even a stone wall.
> Son of Lugalbanda, Gilgamesh, perfect in strength,
> Son of the lofty cow, the wild cow Ninsun.
> He is Gilgamesh, perfect in splendor,
> Who opened up passes in the mountains,
> Who could dig pits even in the mountainside,
> Who crossed the ocean, the broad seas, as far as the sunrise.

Gilgamesh, part human, part divine (since his mother is the wild cow goddess, Ninsun), has all the attributes of a proper mythological figure—fierce as a bull, strong as a wave—but also possesses the practical skills valued by your down-to-earth Sumerian businessman: he is a terrific engineer and an incomparable navigator. And this winning combination of qualities gives us a hint that the story of Gilgamesh is the result of a long process of development and maturation. It may easily have arisen in a past so remote—long before writing, even long before agriculture—that no archaeologist can recapture it. But it has been turned and turned like pottery and elaborately decorated by successive hands, first prehistoric, then Sumerian, then Semitic.

The lines I have quoted come from an unbroken portion of Tablet I. But now I must quote from a portion of the tablet that will give a better idea of the difficulties faced by a translator—lines that also suggest that even in lordly Uruk Gilgamesh was a bit much:

In Uruk the Sheepfold he would walk about,
Show himself superior, his head held high like a wild bull.
He had no rival, at his *pukku*
His weapons would rise up, his comrades have to rise up.
The young men of Uruk became dejected in their private
    [quarters(?)].
Gilgamesh would not leave any son alone for his father.
Day and night his [behavior(?)] was overbearing. . . .
He is the shepherd of Uruk the Sheepfold,
He is their shepherd, yet [   ]
Powerful, superb, knowledgeable, [and expert],
Gilgamesh would not leave young girls [alone],
The daughters of warriors, the brides of young men.

"At his *pukku*" may mean "alert" or "erect" or it may refer to a kind of hockey game associated with fertility and played at weddings. The translator's brackets mark places where the tablet is broken or unclear. The young men may have become dejected in their private quarters or in their private thoughts—we can't be sure. But despite the lacunae and untranslatable words, we can be pretty sure that Gilgamesh was making a nuisance of himself, bullying the boys and bedding the girls. And this seems to be seen by the Sumerians as the necessary excrescence of greatness. Sumerian society, we know from other tablets, was intensely competitive, and Sumerians were swaggerers of the worst kind. Kings indulged in their own constant self-praise without a trace of inhibition. The citizenry often resorted to the law courts, whose "verdicts" fill many tablet collections as one of the most pervasive literary forms. Another pervasive form, which the Sumerians found especially entertaining, is the "contest," a fanciful public disputation between two rivals—between, for instance, two schoolboys over who is the better student (a disputation replete with such appellations as "dolt," "numbskull," "illiterate," and "windbag"); between two suitors for the hand of a goddess; even between copper and silver, summer and winter. This was a society full of contentiousness and aggression, in which the "good" man—the ideal—was imagined as ambitious in the extreme, animated by a drive for worldly prestige, victory, success, with scant regard to what we would think of as ethical norms. This was also a society that despised poverty.

At any rate, the people of Uruk, for all their pride in Gilgamesh, need some relief, and so they complain bitterly to their gods, especially to "great Aruru," the universal mother:

> "Did [Aruru (?)] create such a rampant wild bull?
> Is there no rival? . . .
> You, Aruru, you created [mankind (?)]!
> Now create someone for him, to match (?) the ardor (?) of
>   his energies!
> Let them be regular rivals, and let Uruk be allowed peace!"

So Aruru creates "inside herself the word of Anu," the father god. Then, washing her hands, she pinches "off a piece of clay, cast[s] it out in open country," where it becomes "Enkidu, the warrior, offspring of silence, and sky-bolt of Ninurta":

> His whole body was shaggy with hair, he was furnished with
>   tresses like a woman,
> His locks of hair grew luxuriant like grain.
> He knew neither people nor country; he was dressed as
>   cattle are.
> With gazelles he eats vegetation,
> With cattle he quenches his thirst at the watering place.
> With wild beasts he satisfies his need for water.

Enkidu, the ultimate "natural man," at one with animals rather than humans, foils the strategies of the local hunters, one of whom brings the hunters' complaints to Gilgamesh:

"I am too frightened to approach him.
He kept filling in the pits that I dug [   ],
He kept pulling out the traps that I laid.
He kept helping cattle, wild beasts of open country, to
    escape my grasp."

Gilgamesh's solution is remarkable:

"Go, hunter, lead forth the harlot Shamhat,
And when he approaches the cattle at the watering place,
She must take off her clothes, reveal her attractions.
He will see her and go close to her.
Then his cattle, who have grown up in open country with
    him, will become alien to him."

The hunter does as Gilgamesh bids, bringing Shamhat to
the watering place; and when Enkidu, "the murderous
youth from the depths of open country," arrives to drink
with the wild beasts:

Shamhat loosened her undergarments, opened her legs and
    he took in her attractions.
She did not pull away. She took wind of him,
Spread open her garments, and he lay upon her.
She did for him, the primitive man, as women do.
His love-making he lavished upon her.
For six days and seven nights Enkidu was aroused and
    poured himself into Shamhat.
When he was sated with her charms,

He set his face towards the open country of his cattle.
The gazelles saw Enkidu and scattered,
The cattle of open country kept away from his body.
For Enkidu had become smooth; his body was too clean.
His legs, which used to keep pace with his cattle, were at a
     standstill.
Enkidu had been diminished, he could not run as before.
Yet he had acquired judgment (?), had become wiser.

Dumbfounded by this transformation, Enkidu returns to the harlot to find out what this is all about. She tells him that he has "become like a god" and urges that his proper place is now in Uruk,

"Where Gilgamesh is perfect in strength,
And is like a wild bull, more powerful than (any of) the
     people."
She spoke to him, and her speech was acceptable.
Knowing his own mind (now),* he would seek for a friend.

Of course, Enkidu's way of "seek[ing] for a friend" is unusual:

"Let me challenge him, and [   ]
(By saying:) 'In Uruk I shall be the strongest!'
I shall go in and alter destiny:
One who was born in open
     country has [superior (?)]
     strength!"

_____
* In addition to brackets, the
translator uses parentheses to indicate
where she is making the implicit
explicit or engaging in speculative
reconstruction.

But Gilgamesh has already been alerted to the coming of Enkidu by symbolic dreams, which have been interpreted for him by his mother, Ninsun:

". . . a strong partner shall come to you, one who can save
    the life of a friend,
He will be the most powerful in strength of arms in the
    land.
His strength will be as great as that of a sky-bolt of Anu.
You will love him as a wife, you will dote upon him.
[And he will always] keep you safe (?)."

Shamhat knows of Gilgamesh's dreams and their interpretation and relates these to Enkidu, concluding:

"[The dreams mean that you will lo]ve one another."

Tablet II, on which the story continues, is full of gaps, but it is clear that Enkidu, on arriving in Uruk, does challenge Gilgamesh and "they grappled,"

Wrestled in the street, in the public square.
Doorframes shook, walls quaked.

Then, upon the intervention of Ninsun, a weeping Gilgamesh makes a speech that is, given the present state of the text, largely incomprehensible. But

Enkidu stood, listened to him speaking,
Pondered, and then sat down, began to cry.
His eyes grew dim with tears.
His arms slackened, his strength [(   )]
(Then) they grasped one another,
Embraced and held (?) hands.

The mystery of this long-departed people is made even more mysterious by the lacunae in this text. But a couple of things are clear: as in all warrior societies of the Bronze and Iron Ages, the most valued human relationships are between males (and, whether or not such relationships are actively sexual, they must surely be deemed, precisely, homosexual— that is, of the same sex); for all this, congress with a woman is, somehow, civilizing—that is, anti-animalizing, rendering a man ready for the life of the city—for it is because of his encounter with Shamhat that Enkidu is alienated from nature and made ready for entry into Uruk.* As for Shamhat's harlotry, she is obviously not a common harlot: she is given far too much prestige, being party to the king's dreams and his most intimate conversations with his mother. Most likely, she is one of the company of holy harlots, sacred prostitutes consecrated to the worship of one of the gods and ritually (and regularly) ravished by a high priest within the temple pre-

---

* This civilizing, which only contact with a woman can accomplish, has much in common with the civilizing, brilliantly limned by Leslie Fiedler in *Love and Death in the American Novel,* in which he discerns mythological dimensions in such characters as Aunt Sally in *Huckleberry Finn,* one of the many "civilizing" women of American literature whom all full-blooded males must escape as they head off for male bonding in the wilderness.

cincts. Likewise, the repeated epithets used to describe En-kidu—"word of Anu," "sky-bolt of Ninurta," "axe"—appear to be, as the translator Stephanie Dalley puts it delicately, "puns on terms for cult personnel of uncertain sexual affinities who were found particularly in Uruk, associated with Ishtar's cult"—in other words, sacred male prostitutes.

Gilgamesh and Enkidu, now fast friends, more closely bound than husband and wife, having vowed to defend each other even to death, set out to slay the monster Humbaba, an almost unimaginably terrifying creature whose face looks like coiled intestines and

. . . whose shout is the flood-weapon, whose utterance is
   Fire, whose breath is Death,
Can hear for a distance of sixty leagues through (?) the . . .
   of the forest, so who can penetrate his forest?

But, coos the mighty warrior Gilgamesh,

"Hold my hand, my friend, let us set off!
Your heart shall soon burn (?) for conflict; forget death and
   [think only of] life (?).
Man is strong, prepared to fight, responsible.
He who goes in front (and) guards his (friend's) body, shall
   keep the comrade safe.
They shall have established fame for their [future (?)]."

With Enkidu's help, Gilgamesh slays the monster—very dirty work—after which the king cleans himself up and attires himself in robes, "manly sash," and crown. Looking good, he attracts the attention of Ishtar, goddess of love and war:

"Come to me, Gilgamesh, and be my lover!
Bestow on me the gift of your fruit!
You shall be my husband, and I can be your wife."

But Gilgamesh knows that the goddess has had many mates, all of whom she eventually disposed of. "Which of your lovers lasted forever?" asks Gilgamesh.

"Which of your masterful paramours went to heaven?
Come, let me [describe (?)] your lovers to you!"

Gilgamesh then catalogues Ishtar's many companions and their sad fate at her hands (she is, after all, the goddess of love *and* war), starting with the shepherd Dumuzi, with whom Gilgamesh feels a close identification:

"For Dumuzi the lover of your youth
You decreed that he should keep weeping year after year."

Dumuzi, Sumerian mythology's great dying god—like Osiris in Egypt, Adonis in Greece, and many others—was particularly beloved of ordinary people, who interpreted the dramatic cycle of the seasons as his annual death (his "weeping year after year") and resurrection. So moved were they by his fate that they would sit and weep for him during the rains of winter. It may well be that Dumuzi's story is a faint memory of a time when Sumer's kings, imagined as consorts of a goddess, were periodically sacrificed to ensure fertility, as were kings in other ancient societies.

Gilgamesh ends his catalogue of Ishtar's lovers with a story similar to Dumuzi's, that of another force of fertility, the garden god Ishullanu, whose inventions were responsible for much of the beauty of Sumer's cities:

"You loved Ishullanu, your father's gardener,
Who was always bringing you baskets of dates.
They brightened your table every day;
You lifted your eyes to him and went to him
'My own Ishullanu, let us enjoy your strength,
So put out your hand, touch our vulva!'
But Ishullanu said to you,
'Me? What do you want of me?
Did my mother not bake for me, and did I not eat?
What I eat (with you) would be loaves of dishonor and
    disgrace,
Rushes would be my only covering against the cold.'
You listened as he said this,
You hit him, turned him into a frog (?),
Left him to stay amid the fruits of his labors.

But the pole (?) goes up no more, [his bucket] goes down
   no more.*
And how about me? You will love me and then [treat me]
   just like them!"

Ishtar, furious at Gilgamesh, who has "spelled out to me
my dishonor, my dishonor and my disgrace," ascends to
heaven and convinces the father god to send down the Bull of
Heaven to destroy Gilgamesh. But together Gilgamesh and
Enkidu overcome the unconquerable Bull and butcher it. For
this impiety, one of the friends must die, and Enkidu is
chosen by the Council of Heaven. Why Enkidu? The text of
the tablets, so often repetitive and meandering (much more
so than is apparent from my terse summaries), turns unchar-
acteristically compact and understated. But there may be a
suggestion that Gilgamesh deflects the malign attention of the
gods because he has a patronal god all his own—his dead
father Lugalbanda, whose portable effigy he anoints while
dedicating to him the spoils of the Bull's enormous horns,
now splendidly decorated with "thirty minas of lapis lazuli"
and sheathed with "two minas of gold." This homage to an
ancestor or other household god, whose presence was localized in a small image, was a ritual of many ancient societies.

At Enkidu's death, Gilgamesh sets up a wailing hymn of
mourning, more tender than we
might think this earliest civilization capable of, asking for tears
from all the orders of human be-

---

* Like all early peoples, the
Sumerians delighted in puns and
double entendre. This reference to
the *shadoof* technique of irrigation is
also a reference to sex.

ings that make up the city of Uruk, from the wild beasts and even from the trees, thus exalting Enkidu to the status (and even, to some extent, to the identity) of the pathetic, beloved Dumuzi. Gilgamesh ends with the same gesture Achilles will make many centuries later in the *Iliad* on the death of his companion-in-arms Patroclus:

> "Turn to me, you! You aren't listening to me!
> But he cannot lift his head.
> I touch his heart, but it does not beat at all."

Gilgamesh weeps over the body of Enkidu for six days and seven nights, allowing him to be buried only after "a worm fell out of his nose."

Enkidu, like all who die, has gone down to Kur, a dark, dreary, pleasureless place on the far side of a river where a ferryman—just like Charon in the later Greek myth of Hades—transports the naked and enervated souls of the dead to their final haunt, where "vermin eat [them] like an old blanket," where one "sits in a crevice full of dust." (The picture is not unlike the one that medieval artists will paint of hell.) Gilgamesh resolves to avoid the common human fate by obtaining the secret of immortality. But only one mortal man has been granted immortality: Ut-napishtim. This figure of Sumerian mythology, the model for Noah in the later biblical narrative, was found virtuous enough to be given the divine guidance to save his family and a remnant of all living things by building an ark in the primordial time of the universal flood, when the gods decided to destroy the human race.

After horrifying adventures among the Scorpion-men, "whose aura is frightful and whose glance is death," great Gilgamesh succeeds in reaching an alewife who can give him directions to the paradise of Dilmun, where "Ut-napishtim and his woman are as gods," living forever. But in one especially well-preserved version, the alewife has her own sage advice to give:

"Gilgamesh, where do you roam?
You will not find the eternal life you seek.
When the gods created mankind
They appointed death for mankind,
Kept eternal life in their own hands.
So, Gilgamesh, let your stomach be full,
Day and night enjoy yourself in every way,
Every day arrange for pleasures.
Day and night, dance and play,
Wear fresh clothes.
Keep your head washed, bathe in water,
Appreciate the child who holds your hand,
Let your wife enjoy herself in your lap."

After battling "the things of stone," Gilgamesh finally reaches Ut-napishtim "the far-distant"; and this Sumerian Noah has even blunter advice:

"[Why (?)] have you exerted yourself? What have you achieved (?)?

You have made yourself weary for lack of sleep,
You only fill your flesh with grief,
You only bring the distant days (of reckoning) closer.
Mankind's fame is cut down like reeds in a reed-bed.
A fine young man, a fine girl,
[   ] of Death.
Nobody sees Death,
Nobody sees the face of Death,
Nobody hears the voice of Death.
Savage Death just cuts mankind down.
Sometimes we build a house, sometimes we make a nest,
But then brothers divide it upon inheritance.
Sometimes there is hostility [in the land],
But then the river rises and brings flood-water.
Dragonflies drift on the river,
Their faces look upon the face of the Sun,
(But then) suddenly there is nothing.
The sleeping (?) and the dead are just like each other,
Death's picture cannot be drawn. . . .
The Anunnaki, the great gods, assembled; . . .
They appointed death and life.
They did not mark out days for death,
But they did so for life."

On these sober words, which appear to constitute the
main lesson of the *Epic,* we take our leave of Gilgamesh, but
not without drawing some conclusions from what we have
read. Though the casual reader may easily identify certain

Sumerian qualities—such as love of invention and admiration of those who are unabashedly competitive—as qualities that are valued in our own society, one misses much if one fails to notice how differently these qualities play in the ancient context. Inventions are the property of the gods—as are human beings, who have been created to be servants of the gods and to offer them assuaging sacrifices. The aggression of the great warrior lords, like Gilgamesh, and the strong bonds of solidarity between warriors are supremely necessary to the city-states of Sumer, which, though they belong to a single, unified culture, war with one another constantly, as will the later city-states of Greece, always jockeying for some advantage one over the other. But there can be no permanent victory, for either city or warrior. Even the gods are often at odds with one another; and Gilgamesh survives despite the wishes of outraged Ishtar probably because he has the protection of two gods, the wise wild cow who is his mother and the now-deified Lugalbanda, his father. But who can say when a human being will trespass against one of the many gods and incur doom? And even if one should escape such a fate, Death, the end of happiness, is inescapable.

There are faint echoes in the *Epic of Gilgamesh* of notes that will sound more forcefully and coherently in the Epic of Israel, the early books of the Hebrew Bible, which, though they will be written down in a later time and in a somewhat different place, grow out of this time and place. The strongest of these is the theme of the primordial flood and the ark, which saves from destruction the just remnant of the living.* Ut-napishtim and his wife, who have become "as gods" in the garden paradise of Dilmun, may also remind us of Adam and Eve, whose desire to become "as gods" precipitates their exile from a garden called "Eden"—a name which may itself be a borrowing from the Sumerian. And Shamhat's reassurance to Enkidu that his humanization has made him more "like a god" reminds us of the assertion in the Book of Genesis that humans are created, unlike animals, "in the image of God." And Enkidu was created, like the creation in Genesis, by the word of the father god and, like Adam, was molded from clay.

Among the fainter echoes of our Bible that we may discern in these most ancient records is the language of love that Ishtar employs, not unlike the language of the Song of Songs. The "Council of Heaven" reminds us of many biblical phrases in which God seems to take counsel with other divine beings or with angels and in which heaven is envisioned as a royal court. The descriptions of the realm of the dead are reminiscent not only of the Greek Hades but of the Jewish Sheol. The waters of the flood are described as rising up from the primordial Chaos that surrounds the Heaven-Earth, the universe laid out by the gods, in a manner very like the Chaos that surrounds God's emerging creation at the outset of Genesis. And the worldly-wise advice of Ut-napishtim and the alewife

* The discovery of this earlier Sumerian "Noah" in the first attempts to translate cuneiform tablets toward the end of the nineteenth century raised as much anxiety as Darwin did among Victorians, who had assumed that everything in the Bible was without antecedent because it was the "Word of God."

must prompt us to think of the Bible's Wisdom books, especially Ecclesiastes with its cynical, world-weary tone.

One theme that belongs to Gilgamesh but is nowhere to be found among the books of the Bible is fertility—or, rather, its timbre is so different as to make it unrecognizable. The temple of Ishtar, awesomely dominating the heights of Uruk, scene of sacred sexual rites involving orders of prostitutes both male and female, harks back to a world even older than Uruk, a world in which human copulation was seen as the localized expression of the cosmic Heaven-Earth, the great fertility machine created by the gods, who were themselves the archetypal—and highly sexed—engenderers of all that is.

W̶e have looked on Uruk, this city of baked brick rising from the banks of the Euphrates in the intense heat of the Mesopotamian sun, we have imagined its society and listened to some of the many-told tales that were the staple of its entertainment. Now let's delve into the deepest level of the Sumerian psyche—to the ultimate beliefs that held this society together, to the spiritual matrix that created the Sumerian worldview. In order to delve deeper we must, paradoxically, climb higher. For we must ascend the lofty stair and enter the great temple overlooking the heights of another Sumerian city—the Temple of the Moon, acropolis of the city of Ur, ancient imperial capital of Sumer. As we make our way to the center of mystery, we need to ask some basic questions about this place.

Why were all early temples and sacred places built at the highest point available to the builders? Because this is the place nearest the sky. And why is the most sacred space nearest the sky? Because the sky is the divine opposite of life on earth, home of all that is eternal in contrast to the mortal life of earth. When primitive man looked up at the heavens, he saw a vast cavalcade of divine figures regularly passing before his eyes—the cosmic drama, breathtaking in its eternal order and predictability. Here are the eternal prototypes and models for mortal life; but a great gulf yawns between the two spheres, for the life of the heavens, the life of the gods, is immortal and everlasting, while life in the earthly sphere is mortal, ending in death. For the earliest human beings—the first creatures to look upon the drama of the heavens with comprehension—these insights required little reasoning and no discussion; they were immediate and obvious, self-evident truths. This meditation on the heavens was the aboriginal religious experience. In the words of the preeminent modern scholar of religion Mircea Eliade: "The phrase 'contemplating the vault of heaven' really means something when it is applied to primitive man, receptive to the miracles of every day to an extent we find it hard to imagine. Such contemplation is the same as a revelation. The sky shows itself as it really is: infinite, transcendent. The vault of heaven is, more than anything else, 'something quite apart' from the tiny thing that is man and his span of life. The symbolism of its transcendence derives from the simple realization of its infinite height. 'Most high' becomes quite naturally an attribute of the divinity. The regions above man's reach, the starry places, are invested with the divine majesty of the transcendent, of absolute reality, of everlastingness. Such places are the dwellings of the gods; certain privileged people [like Lugalbanda] go there as a result of rites effecting their ascension into heaven. . . . The 'high' is something inaccessible to man as such; it belongs by right to superhuman powers and beings; when a man ceremonially ascends the steps of a sanctuary, or the ritual ladder leading to the sky, he ceases to be a man."

As we continue to climb to the sanctuary, the primeval worldview of the people who built the steps we tread becomes ever more evident. The cosmology of the Sumerians was based on perceptions of societies, now irretrievably ancient, that had preceded them; and, with a few adjustments, it would be received as truth by almost all societies that followed the Sumerians, right down to the threshold of modern times. Earth was a flat circle, attached at its perimeter to the dome of Heaven. Between Earth and Heaven was the element of Air, in which, high up, hung the astral bodies passing before the eyes of Earth-dwellers, pictorial projections of the drama of Heaven, which was also of course predictive of life on Earth, itself a kind of weak imitation of the heavenly drama. Just beneath the circle of Earth was the realm of Death—Hades, Sheol, the shadowy hell to which the dead were consigned—a sort of basement of the Sea of Chaos that surrounded the Earth-Heaven on all sides, whence rain fell and flood rose. Each of these great elements was a god: Heaven was father; Earth was mother; Air, which contained the eternal but ever-revolving pictures of the cosmic drama and clues (for the insightful interpreter) to our life on Earth, was mediator between Heaven and Earth and therefore the most important god in the Sumerian pantheon; and the Sea was necessarily an unpredictable and troubling ally, to be treated with caution.

But let us approach the sacred precincts of the Moon, the apparition in the night sky that, more than any other, fascinated ancient peoples. Even today, a policeman in any city on earth will tell you that crime increases under the full moon and that "lunatics"—those who are made demented by the moon (*luna* in Latin)—are then much more active and troublesome. Midwives and veterinarians are convinced that the full moon induces labor, and, even in the most secular of cities, hospital labor rooms are as overwhelmed with females toiling to bring their young to birth on the night of a full moon as are barns in rural hamlets. Nor can anyone deny the awesome power of attraction that the moon exercises over the tides of ocean and sea, as the great body in the night sky beams its ethereal light on the roiling waters.

We climb the last steps to the entrance, passing sculptured serpents with glowing eyes of lapis lazuli. We pass the pillared facade of the vestibule and enter the inner courtyard, where we can see dimly, through a series of archways, the distant image of the Moon god, flickering in the lights of hundreds of votive flames. The walls of the courtyard are decorated with cones of red, black, and tan, which create precise geometric patterns—triangles, lozenges, zigzags, and spirals. At last we enter the sanctuary of Nanna-Sin, Moon god of the Sumerians, whose impassive statue now looms above us, rigid and enormous-eyed, its polychrome pupils emptily burning. Behind the statue a monumental moon is frescoed on the wall, surrounded by a slithering snake. Within the orb of the moon a gigantic black spider spreads its spindly legs. As our nostrils take in the pungent clouds of incense, our ears detect a hissing sound: around the feet of Nanna-Sin, pythons, brightly marked with black and orange lozenge patterns, coil and uncoil their scaly bodies in slow motion. We are distracted from Sin's unyielding visage by a buzz of movement just in front of us, where on a modest waist-high altar of baked brick, surrounded by a swarm of flies, the largest python is devouring the fetus of a donkey, whose blood runs down in rivulets along neatly scooped-out gutters to collection bowls at the altar's base. Involuntarily, we take a step backward, as the smell of warm blood and entrails combines with the suffocating incense. Gasping for air, we retreat to the courtyard.

But tonight is the night of the full moon; and, as darkness quickly falls and the moon rises in the heavens, we hear the sounds of hundreds of priestesses, chanting dully and playing primitive pipes and drums. Dressed in elaborate ceremonial garb, they gather solemnly around the terrace on which the temple is built, looking upward to the stepped pyramid beyond the temple, which rises almost in defiance of geometry, almost (it seems) to the sky itself. At the highest platform of this ziggurat (for so the stepped pyramid is called) is a small but glowing altar of lapis lazuli, carved fantastically with snakes and giant spiders, to which an adolescent boy has been bound on his back. He is naked, though his flesh has been decorated in patterns of lozenges and zigzags to resemble the cobra. Priestesses of the highest order, also naked except for their extraordinary rings and spiral bracelets, are massaging the boy with gentle foreplay. As the moonlight illuminates his swelling member, the high priestess appears, as if from nowhere, dressed in a silver garment, which she sheds. Now naked, except for the myriad pearls that decorate her body and the painted spirals that adorn her breasts, she mounts the boy with the assistance of her sisters, who shriek their encouragement in a frenzy that only grows higher as the high priestess rides the boy, at first with rhythmic dignity, then with increasing agitation till her pearls tremble in the moonlight like so many minuscule planets, and the lozenges and spirals glisten, and both bodies, writhing in sweat, appear to be not so much earthly bodies as inhuman forces of the cosmos. All the priestesses, the lowest orders still on the terrace at the ziggurat's base, the higher orders arranged in ascending importance on the lofty steps of the ziggurat itself, are growing wild and ecstatic. Ripping open their robes and pawing themselves, they bay upward to the event on the ziggurat's height and to the moon itself.

At such a moment, unnoticed visitors from another time and place might well grow lightheaded and faint. Let us suppose that by the time we revive, we are alone on a terrace illuminated by the ghostly light of the full moon. We look up at the ziggurat, surmounted by its empty altar of vivid blue, and wonder if we have imagined it all.

What I have just attempted is a reconstruction which any scholar could fault in one detail or another. The Sumerian temples and ziggurats, exposed to the wear of millennia, are in far worse repair than the tablets; but taking an extant bit of one sacred precinct and combining it with an extant bit of another, I think I have described fairly accurately a *possible* Temple of the Moon and its accompanying ziggurat. As for the ceremony of the full moon, we really don't know much about its details, though we do know that ceremonies were conducted throughout Sumer to celebrate the phases of the moon and that they were conducted with high seriousness. We know also that the Moon cult was centered on Ur, Sumer's usual capital (though the capital moved around depending on which city was dominant at a particular time), and we know that sacred couplings (or "marriages") were a staple of Sumerian ritual, that there were sacred priest-prostitutes both male and female, and that the *en* (or high priest) of a temple and the *en*'s retinue were always the sex opposite to the sex of the god worshiped there. Nanna-Sin, the Sumerian Moon god, was male, so his temple was staffed by priestesses. At Uruk, where Ishtar, the fickle goddess of love, was especially worshiped, her temple was staffed by male priests, and the king himself (as stand-in for Dumuzi) had congress with a sacred female prostitute or priestess (as stand-in for Ishtar) every New Year to ensure the fertility of the kingdom during the planting, growing, and harvest seasons. To this ceremony all the officials of the city bore witness in serried ranks. Whether the Mysteries of the Moon were public (open to the whole population of the city-state) or semiprivate (as I have described) or carried out in extreme privacy, we cannot say. But there is no reason to think that the Sumerians, who liked to picture the water god Enki rampant, supporting an enormous erection while ejaculating the Tigris, were shy about sexual matters; and it may well be that the rite I have described was far more orgiastic and involved multiple couplings and a large cast of both sexes. What I would really like to know more about is the ravished prostitute: was he/she bred to this fate or taken as a battle hostage? After the event was he/she made a permanent part of the temple priesthood or sacrificed like an animal—as the king of Uruk himself may have been, at least in earliest times, in liturgical imitation of the vegetation god Dumuzi? We just don't know; but we do know that human sacrifice was not beyond the Sumerians, for archaeologists have dug up the burial chambers of dead kings who were entombed with all their family, household, and retinue.

If we could go backward in time to ancient Sumer, like characters in a Steven Spielberg film, we would find this culture attractive and even titillating, but then alienating and even repulsive, and finally frightening and even dangerous. Human life, seen as a pale reenactment of the life of the eternal heavens, was ruled by a fate beyond the pitifully limited powers of human beings. The gods decided. The figures in the heavens, if interpreted aright by those who had access to secret priestly knowledge and whom the society supported in leisure, could give some indication of what would happen next in earthly affairs. But one's fate was written in the stars and could not be changed.

And no figure in the heavens was more important than

the moon, that heavenly image of earthly life, which was born, waxed, waned, and died, just as we do, and then returned in new life, just as happens in the earthly realm. But I do not return, do I? This question would have had little meaning in Sumer, even though its great hero Gilgamesh tried to find an answer to the anguish that lies behind the question. There were no rounded individuals in Sumer, just temporary, earthly images of heavenly exemplars, patterns, and paradigms, which is why the two-dimensional characters of Sumerian stories display so little individuality. I do not return, of course, any more than does a stalk of grain. But fields of grain return, and so does human life. This is the reason that the sacred prostitutes, the victims of the rituals, appear so disposable, why we know so little about them or their fate. What did they matter? Their high honor was that they had been chosen to enact the heavenly drama on earth. Like the potent lovers of Ishtar, they had served their purpose.

Long before the cities of Sumer had risen above the Tigris and Euphrates, long before farming and herding had been thought of, the first earthly beings to look up at the sky with attention and intelligence had thought these thoughts. The perception of the contingent life of earth as a fleeting reflection of the eternal life of the heavens, the insight that the moon especially mirrors our earthly condition of birth, copulation, and personal death—and then regenera-

THE PRIMEVAL RELIGIOUS EXPERIENCE

tion of species—such thoughts express mankind's original religious experience and form the foundation for all the world's most ancient religions.

For some prehistoric cultures the moon was female, for others it was male, but always was it closely associated with the bodies of women, which like the moon progressed through monthly cycles; and these were cycles of fertility, like those of the earth itself, which many cultures believed was made of the same substance as the moon, was even the moon's child.*

In order to appreciate the prehistoric worldview, we must start with the limitless sky and the overwhelming impression that its recurring drama, especially in the dreamtime of darkest night ("the nocturnal domain of the mind," as Eliade calls it), made on primitive people. They wandered an earth sparsely populated by the human species but otherwise teeming with contingent life (and daily reminders of death and regeneration), an earth so obviously coupled with an unattainable and limitless heaven. What their minds saw as self-evidently so were *correspondences:* women are like the moon and both are like the earth; but women are born and die, whereas the moon lasts forever. The moon is, therefore, the eternal figure of mutability, the exemplar "out there." Likewise, each of the other heavenly bodies—the sun, the constellations, the constant planets—provides us

* The theory proposed by Marija Gimbutas and other feminist archaeologists that the Great Mother was the original god of mankind is almost certainly wrong. Heaven and its spectacles were the first objects of devotion and deification. The Earth goddess, though of tremendous importance and always the complement of Heaven, probably came to special prominence with the invention of agriculture.

with some everlasting exemplar of corruptible earthly life, which has its seasons, its predictable deaths, and regenerations. High heaven is the realm of the father god, whose rain fertilizes like sperm. But whereas heaven is the realm of the eternal, earth is the realm of death, the realm not of exemplars but of mortal examples. The seed must die if the wheat is to grow, just as all living things grow out of corruption, just as all future life must begin with the sacrifice of present life, and all earthly life must end in death.

We may consider naive the absolute confidence of primitive peoples in the rightness of their interpretations of reality. But we should not forget that their sense of correspondence is founded on metaphor (as in a poetic phrase like "the vault of heaven") and that metaphor is the basis of all language and thought, as it is of all religion. Language almost certainly began as a metaphorical enterprise—probably in the human attempt to mimic certain sounds, so that, for instance, the sounds "ma-ma," a form of which all languages use for "mother," began as an imitation of the sucking sound a baby makes at the breast. Deep within each of us, the need for correspondence remains—which is *au fond* the need to perceive ourselves as belonging to the cosmos. This is why something inside us responds spontaneously to metaphor, the heart of all poetry and, finally, of all language and all meaning. When we hear unexpectedly such a phrase as "The silver apples of the moon, the golden apples of the sun" or "My love is like a red, red rose," we experience a distinctively human thrill, the thrill of hearing language at its most concentrated.

Perhaps the sky no longer seems, to most of us, a revolving picture of the gods; perhaps it is not, except to those who cast horoscopes, exemplary or predictive of life on earth. But it is still our principal metaphor for limitlessness and transcendence. In a fundamental, ineradicable way, we still see with the eyes of our earliest ancestors and our hearts still quicken to the same things theirs did.

TWO

THE JOURNEY
IN THE DARK

✴

The Unaccountable Innovation

In the revolving drama of the heavens, primitive peoples saw an immortal, wheel-like pattern that was predictive of mortal life. At the center of this Wheel of Life they found the Hub of Death. The correspondences they discerned between earthly and heavenly realities are pictured in their earliest art—the spirals, zigzags, and lozenges, abounding almost everywhere in the most ancient monuments left to us. The spiral, ever turning, ever beginning again, is the image of the cyclical nature of reality—of the phases of the moon, the changing of the seasons, the cycle of a woman's body, the ever-turning Wheel of birth, copulation, and death. The zigzags sometimes represent lightning, which was associated with the moon, because the moon was thought to control all water and fertility—and lightning precedes a storm. But, most anciently, zigzags are the symbols of flowing water, found on neolithic pottery and among the oldest hieroglyphs of Egypt. The lozenge, or diamond shape, is the ancient symbol for the vulva, which would one day be reduced to a cleft triangle and become the aboriginal Sumerian pictograph for "woman." Recently, there was discovered in Australia what may turn out to be the earliest human art: a series of circles engraved on a 130-foot sandstone monolith that takes us back seventy-five thousand years—archaic man's first acknowledgment of the Great Pattern that he read everywhere, the ever-turning Wheel.

Religion is a complex phenomenon; and the correspondences soon became more complex, requiring orders of priests and shamans for their correct interpretation and effective use. The phallic snake, which sheds its skin and also disappears for part of each year, and thus was thought to die and regenerate itself, became in many different cultures the moon's earthly manifestation. Idols recovered from such widely distant places as the Panchan and Ngan-Yang cultures of neolithic China and the Amerindian civilization of Calchaqui show the lozenge-decorated serpent, male and female combined, symbol of dualism reintegrated and potent predictor of fertility. Another moon-creature was the spider, whose silvery, cyclical web traps its victims in an image of man's fate, which the moon, who sways all living things, was thought to control. (To spin is to predestine; and some of the oldest words for fate, such as the Anglo-Saxon *wyrd,* come from the Indo-European verb *uert,* meaning "to turn" or "to spin.") The bull, whose crescent horns are the very image of the sickle moon, was sacred to Nanna-Sin, who was himself "the powerful calf with strong horns," "the young bull of the sky." The pearl was the Moon god's amulet, the shining little moon contained within the vulva of the oyster. In pre-Columbian Mexico the snail, which like the moon, displays and withdraws its horns, was sacred to the moon, as was in Ice Age Europe the bear, who appears and disappears with the seasons and is the ancestor of humanity. Among peoples as widely dispersed as the African Bushmen, the Samoyed, and the Chinese, a whole series of lunar figures who were missing a hand or foot (like the incomplete moon) were

THE EVOLUTION OF WRITING

(1) The pictograph in the top row originally represents "star" but also comes to designate "god." (2) The cleft triangle (which had an even more ancient antecedent, the lozenge or diamond shape) stands for the female genitals but also comes to designate "woman." (3) Mountains. (4) "Mountain woman," that is, a Semitic slave girl.

Pictured above (from left to right) is the evolution of each sign from an original pictograph into a more easily incised symbol, shaped by the strokes of a small wedge-shaped stylus—thus cuneiform (or wedge-shaped) writing.

characterized by their power to bring rain and subsequent fertility.

In examining these correspondences that primitive man found so obvious, we post-Aristotelians are more likely to be struck by their illogic than by their appositeness. To see with the eyes of primitive society, we must abandon both our logic and our science. "The point," writes Eliade, "of all these analogies is first of all to unite man with the rhythms and energies of the cosmos, and then to unify the rhythms"—as in the sacred copulation rite—"fuse the centers and finally effect a leap into the transcendent," what Eliade calls the "primal unity." The underlying purpose of primitive theology was no different from that of any other human attempt to reach the truth: these people, our distant ancestors, were looking for knowledge that was *effective,* that could help them achieve prosperity, progeny, and the only immortality available to human beings—assurance that their seed would not die with them. And for the more mystical among them, there was the belief that this knowledge could put them in touch with something beyond themselves. Every rite has its irrational, mystical center, its acme of consecration, its moment out of time; and whether it is the transformation of the bread and wine at Mass, the whirling of the dervish, or the orgasm of Sumer, its purpose is ecstatic union, however fleeting, with transcendent reality, with the ultimate, with what is beyond mutability. For the ancients, such reality was beyond earth, beyond even the moon, beyond all becoming. *"Supra lunam sunt aeterna omnia,"* wrote Cicero, echoing a most ancient Mediterranean belief in absolutes: "Beyond the moon are all the eternal things."

A century or two after the beginning of the second millennium B.C., a family of Ur found wanting this static worldview of heavenly absolutes and earthly corruption. They were Terah's family, as we read in Genesis, the first book of the Bible:

Now these are the begettings of Terah:

Terah begot Avram,* Nahor and Haran;

and Haran begot Lot.

Haran died in the living-presence of Terah his father in the
     land of his kindred, in Ur of the Chaldeans.

Avram and Nahor took themselves wives;

The name of Avram's wife was Sarai,

The name of Nahor's wife was Milcah—daughter of Haran,
     father of Milcah and father of Yisca.

Now Sarai was barren, she had no child.

Terah took Avram his son and Lot son of Haran, his son's
     son, and Sarai his daughter-in-law, wife of Avram his son,

They set out together from Ur
     of the Chaldeans, to go to
     the land of Canaan.

But when they had come as far
     as Harran, they settled there.

And the days of Terah were five
     years and two hundred years,
     then Terah died,
     in Harran.

At first glance, this may strike
the reader as an unimpressive
narrative that, in its plainness and
peculiarity (Terah, whoever he
was, did not live for more than
two centuries), has certain affinities with the narratives of Sumer,

* "Avram" is the Abram of most
English translations, who will
eventually become "Avraham"—
Abraham in most translations. I am
using the brilliant new translation of
Genesis made by Everett Fox, which
is much closer to the Hebrew text,
including its spelling, than are most
translations. I normally employ the
spelling of the translator I am
quoting, though I sometimes revert
to the traditional King James spelling
in summary sections. The phrase "of
the Chaldeans" in this passage is an
anachronism, supplied by a scribe to
situate Ur for readers of a later day
when the Euphrates valley had come
to be dominated by Chaldean
Semites (who much later gave their
name to the Chaldean Christian
minority of Iraq). Many such
anachronisms can be found in
Genesis.

if none of their mythological dash. But there are surprising dissimilarities: the careful preserving of the names and lineages of ancient characters—even of women—who were neither gods nor kings; and the importance placed on what *appear* at least to be exacting genealogical records.

Terah's was a family of Semites, long settled at Ur, now "the land of his kindred." His ancestors, hundreds of years earlier, had been part of the movement of wandering Semitic tribes that had overwhelmed the power of Sumer and been subsequently absorbed by its superior urban culture. The lines quoted here, a translation from the Semitic tongue called Hebrew, are found in Genesis just after the stories of human beginnings—from the Creation to the Flood. But unlike the stories that precede it, this chronicle of Terah's family sounds not like a fairy tale but like an attempt at real historical narrative; and though, in this written form, it is probably less than three thousand years old, it is the product of an oral tradition that takes us back almost four thousand years, close to the beginning of the second millennium B.C., to the period of Babylonian Sumer's Golden Age under the aegis of Hammurabi, the world's first emperor.

We cannot be sure what these citizens of Ur had in mind when they set out. Probably not much. They traveled northwest along the Euphrates from Ur to Harran, a city also dedicated to the moon, a sister city of Ur and very like it in outlook—San Francisco to Ur's New York. So their first attempt at relocation may have been only to improve their prospects, and there is some reason to believe that they meant to settle permanently in Harran. For Avram, however, Harran was to be but a stage. What is odd about this passage is the assumption that the family's ultimate destination is to be "the land of Canaan," a hinterland of the Semitic tribes, who (at least in Sumerian caricature) ate their meat raw and didn't even know how to bury their dead. No one whose family was established at Ur would have thought to leave it except for a similar city. So what we may be witnessing here is a migration in the wrong direction, a regression to simpler roots from which the urbanized Semites who had settled in Sumer had been cut off for centuries. But this peculiar migration would change the face of the earth by permanently changing the minds and hearts of human beings.

In Harran, Terah and his family struck it rich; and it was almost certainly in Harran that a voice spoke to Avram and said:

"Go-you-forth
from your land,
from your kindred,
from your father's house,
to the land that I will let you see.
I will make a great nation of you
and will give-you-blessing
and will make your name great.
Be a blessing!
I will bless those who bless you,

he who curses you, I will damn.

All the clans of the soil will find blessing through you!"

So, comments the anonymous narrator, "Avram went." And with him went Lot, Sarai, "all their gain they had gained and the souls they had made in Harran," that is, two extended households on the move once more. But in addition to their family members and chattel, they took their Sumerian outlook. However much of a discontinuity with the past this journey would come to represent, Avram, Sarai, and Lot, their families and slaves were people of Sumer and could no more escape the mind-set of their culture than we can escape ours. Something new is happening here; but it is happening as all things new must happen—in the midst of the old, usual, ordinary reality of what was then daily life. *"Nova ex veteris,"* runs the old Latin paradox. "The new must be born out of the old."

For one thing, this family obviously adhered to Sumerian notions of the importance of business; otherwise it would hardly have occurred to the laconic narrator to mention "all their gain they had gained"—all the wealth they had accumulated during their stay in Harran. We know some of the ideas they brought with them—we can almost X-ray their mental baggage—for we can trace Sumerian religious notions in the earliest writings of the descendants of Avram. The voice that spoke to Avram was his patronal god; and in Avram's mind he may not have been, to begin with, much different from Lugalbanda, Gilgamesh's patronal god, whose statue Gilgamesh anointed for good luck. There were many gods, but each human being had a guardian spirit—an ancestor or angel—charged with taking special care of him. These little gods, represented by amulets and portable statues, were, like all the gods, essentially familial—gods of the person, the family, the city, the tribe—and were jealous and contentious, like all family members. Even if in a particular situation they were not responsible for evil (though sometimes they were), in many situations they were powerless to counter evil—and, in any case, human beings were full of evil. "Man behaves badly," pronounces Ut-napishtim sagely. "Never has a sinless child been born," warns a favorite Sumerian proverb. The way to success was to satisfy the duties of one's cult, whatever those might be—which is why Sumerian temples were described with such precision and liturgies (including orgies and sacred couplings) enacted with such attention. It was by just such attention to cultic detail that Ut-napishtim had been found just; and such acts of piety were a Sumerian's only insurance against the ill will of the gods.

We have already seen in the *Epic of Gilgamesh* some of the many mythological elements that would find their echo in the Bible. (The Gilgamesh story was so powerful that it would also influence the Greek stories that Homer would collect into the *Odyssey* as well as the *Arabian Nights* of medieval Islam.) As late as the sixth century B.C., in the Jerusalem temple itself, Israelite women would sit and weep for the god Dumuzi (Tammuz in the Bible), which the prophet Ezekiel notes with loathing. (The myth of the dying god casts so long a shadow that even today Tammuz is the name for a month in the Jewish calendar.) The family of Terah no doubt took with them on their journey the stories of Sumer about the long-lived ancients and the ill-tempered gods— such as the story about the jealous goddess Ishtar, who had a sacred "tree of life," guarded by a serpent, and the story about the ancestral figure whose unique piety enabled him to save a remnant of life in the great flood. And as the family of Terah looked back over their shoulders to the eastern horizon, the last thing they saw of Sumer was the ziggurat of Harran, that bold Sumerian attempt to scale the heavens that would one day become the fabulous, foolish Tower of Babel in Genesis.

But it is also true that, however "Sumerian" this expedition into the wilderness may have looked to the casual observer, its leader carried with him a brand-new idea. *We* know Avram was heading to Canaan, but did he? It is certain that the mention of Canaan in the summary account of the begettings and travels of Terah and his family is by way of overview and does not necessarily indicate that this destination was actually known to Avram when he started out. There is no reason to think that Avram knew where he was going or anything more than what his god had told him— that he was to "go forth" (the Hebrew imperative *"lekh-lekha"* has an insistent immediacy that English cannot duplicate) on a journey of no return to "the land that I will" show you, that this god would *somehow* make of this childless man "a great nation," and that all humanity would eventually find blessing through him.

So, *"wayyelekh Avram"* ("Avram went")—two of the boldest words in all literature. They signal a complete departure from everything that has gone before in the long evolution of culture and sensibility. Out of Sumer, civilized repository of the predictable, comes a man who does not know where he is going but goes forth into the unknown wilderness under the prompting of his god. Out of Mesopotamia, home of canny, self-serving merchants who use their gods to ensure prosperity and favor, comes a wealthy caravan with no material goal. Out of ancient humanity, which from the dim beginnings of its consciousness has read its eternal verities in the stars, comes a party traveling by no known compass. Out of the human race, which knows in its bones that all its striving must end in death, comes a leader who says he has been given an impossible promise. Out of mortal imagination comes a dream of something new, something better, something yet to happen, something—in the future.

If we had lived in the second millennium B.C., the millennium of Avram, and could have canvassed all the nations of the earth, what would they have said of Avram's journey? In most of Africa and Europe, where prehistoric animism was the norm and artists were still carving and painting on stone the heavenly symbols of the Great Wheel of Life and Death, they would have laughed at Avram's madness and pointed to the heavens, where the life of earth had been plotted from all eternity. His wife is barren as winter, they would say; a man cannot escape his fate. The Egyptians would have shaken their heads in disbelief. "There is none born wise," they would say, repeating the advice of their most cherished wise men. "Copy the forefathers. Teach him what has been said in the past; then he will set a good example." The early Greeks might have told Avram the story of Prometheus, whose quest for the fire of the gods ended in personal disaster. Do not overreach, they would advise; come to resignation. In India, he would be told that time is black, irrational, and merciless. Do not set yourself the task of accomplishing something in time, which is only the dominion of suffering. In China, the now anonymous sages whose thoughts would eventually influence the *I Ching* would caution that there is no purpose in journeys or in any kind of earthly striving; the great thing is to abolish time by escaping from the law of change. The ancestors of the Maya in America would point to their circular calendars, which like those of the Chinese repeat the pattern of years in unvarying succession, and would explain that everything that has been comes around again and that each man's fate is fixed. On every continent, in every society, Avram would have been given the same advice that wise men as diverse as Heraclitus, Lao-Tsu, and Siddhartha would one day give their followers: do not journey but sit; compose yourself by the river of life, meditate on its ceaseless and meaningless flow—on all that is past or passing or to come—until you have absorbed the pattern and have come to peace with the Great Wheel and with your own death and the death of all things in the corruptible sphere.

———

On reaching Canaan, Avram "passed through the land, as far as the Place of Shekhem"—which would become for Avram's descendants a sacred space, for Avram "built a slaughter-site there," a small altar by an oak tree where he could offer animal sacrifices to his god. And here at this resting place, the god for the first time identifies this land as the land of the promise: "I give this land to your seed!" "This land"—the identification is fuzzy; there are no demarcations as yet. But from now on each time the god speaks to Avram over the course of many years, the original promise will gain in concreteness. All the same, during these many years Avram and his people, these sophisticated urbanites, will continue to live without fixed abode or title to any land, will continue to be "sojourners"—which is how they will describe themselves. We may begin to suspect that this benighted troupe of wanderers has been taken in by the force of Avram's personality and that Avram has been sent on a wild goose chase at the prompting of his own disordered brain.

For all that, Avram exhibits a sly resourcefulness that we seldom associate with madmen. When famine strikes Canaan, Avram heads for Egypt—"to sojourn there." But in this even more alien territory, where he must guard not against primitive tribes but against a god-king whom no one can gainsay, Avram hatches a scheme, saying to Sarai his wife:

> "Now here, I know well that you are a woman fair to look
> at. [One can imagine Sarai enjoying this compliment and
> then her face falling as—]

It will be, when the Egyptians see you and say: 'She is his
    wife,'
that they will kill me, but you they will allow to live.
Pray say that you are my sister
so that it may go well with me on your account, that I
    myself may give thanks to you."

Sure enough, Pharaoh sticks Sarai in his harem, her
"brother" Avram receiving in return "sheep and oxen,
donkeys, servants and maids, she-asses and camels."✳
We are never told whether Pharaoh gets around to vio-
lating Sarai, nor does the text give any clue to Sarai's
feelings in the matter. But we are told that Avram's god
"plagued Pharaoh with great plagues" and that somehow
Pharaoh learns the cause. Avram is brought before the
Egyptian king, who utters a memorable *"Ma-zot?!"*
("What's this?!"), an almost comic exclamation of frustra-
tion often heard in modern Israel. Then, in a turn of phrase
not far removed from an old vaudeville routine, Pharaoh
sputters:

"Why did you not tell me that she
    is your wife?
Why did you say: 'She is my sis-
    ter?'
So I took her for myself as a wife.
But now, here is your wife, take
    her and go!"

✳ Most scholars find the biblical
references to domesticated camels in
the time of Avram to be
anachronistic because there is no
extra-biblical evidence that camels
were used regularly as beasts of
burden till about 1000 B.C.; for
other scholars the lack of extra-
biblical evidence is inconclusive.

Off goes Avram, brought as quickly as possible to the Egyptian border by Pharaoh's bouncers, "who escorted him and his wife and *all that was his.*" These being the last words of this episode, the narrator, who is getting a big kick out of recording the little farce, wants us to know that Avram has not only saved his neck but greatly increased his wealth. Then, just in case we've missed the point, he adds at the beginning of the next episode that "Avram traveled up from Egypt" and "was exceedingly heavily laden with livestock, with silver, and with gold." In the Egyptian anecdote Sarai has served only as a pawn whose feelings are of no account: the point is the nomadic progenitor's cleverness at the expense of the Egyptian big wig.

How did powerless Avram, nomadic sojourner in the wilderness of Canaan, ever come in contact with mighty Pharaoh, stationary god-king of Egypt? Almost on the heels of the Egyptian anecdote comes a strangely worded episode that gives us the answer. The famine has passed, and Avram's nephew Lot is now settled in Sodom, one of the "cities of the plain" that may have stood in what is today the southern basin of the Dead Sea. But Avram, refusing city life, has pitched his tent on the west side of the Jordan "by the Oaks of Mamre." Word reaches Avram that Lot has been taken prisoner in the course of a war between two leagues of kings, one of Canaanites, the other of Sumerians:

One who escaped came and told Avram the Hebrew—
he was dwelling by the Oaks of Mamre the Amorite, brother
    of Eshcol and brother of Aner,

they were Avram's covenant-allies.

When Avram heard that his brother [actually nephew]* had
    been taken prisoner,

he drew out his retainers, his house-born slaves, eighteen and
    three hundred, and went in pursuit as far as Dan.

Ma-zot? Avram has 318 slaves, not to mention family
members and other "retainers"? Avram has "covenant-allies," like any great chieftain? Avram, the quixotic quester,
the self-conscious nomad, can organize an army of pursuit
that marches all the way from Mamre (modern Hebron) in
the Canaanite south to Dan in the extreme north, a journey
of some hundred miles? The clue to the correct interpretation of this text lies in its description of Avram as "the Hebrew," a description found nowhere else. This story, though
woven into the fabric of Genesis, comes not from the traditions of the Children of Abraham, who never called themselves "the Hebrews," but from the oral lore of their neighbors. Here we see Avram not through the gentle idealization
of subsequent generations of his heirs, but as he was seen
by his contemporaries. Avram, as the Egyptian episode
has already hinted, was neither rube nor flower child,
seeking sweetness and light in the desert. He was a calculating
clansman who for his own reasons had chosen to leave the
great cities of Sumer for the unsettled life of Canaan, but who
was otherwise taking no chances:

* In the Gilgamesh material,
brackets indicated missing or
damaged portions of the text. Here
they are simply my own
interpolations. Parentheses indicate
the translator's attempt to make the
implicit explicit. Hyphens between
words indicate that the Hebrew is
more concise, usually one word.

he was a powerful chieftain with wealth and men at his disposal.

He succeeds in freeing Lot and then, returning south, binds himself even more closely to the local kings by refusing to share in the spoils of their victory:

"So that you should not say: I made Avram rich.
Nothing for me!
Only what the lads have consumed,
and the share of the men who went with me—Aner, Eshcol,
 and Mamre,
let them take their share."

Avram was no half-crazed, solipsistic idealist but a man among men. Even in his dealings with his god there is a note of the self-confident, calculating desert chieftain, who knows how to deal. When he hears the god's voice speaking the great words "Be not afraid," Avram complains, "What would you give me?—for I am going (to die) accursed," and then goes on to say that he has decided to leave his estate to his chief servant, for "to me you have not given seed." To this indirect accusation, the god replies:

"This one shall not be heir to you,
rather, the one that goes out from your own body . . ."
He brought him outside and said:
"Pray look toward the heavens and count the stars,
can you count them?"

And he said to him:

"So shall your seed be."

Though the heavens continue to be mined for metaphor, they are no longer predictive of anything. It is only the god who can predict; the heavens are reduced to serving him as illustration. This is just fine with Avram: the narrator brings the incident to a close by remarking that Avram—the canny, worldly-wise chieftain that we now know him to be—"trusted in" this god and that the god deemed his trust "as righteous-merit on his part." For this trust we are given no reason other than Avram's insight: this self-reliant man relies on his own judgment to interpret correctly what is going on. Out of an age of tall tales of warriors and kings, all so like one another that they are hard to tell apart, comes this story of a skeptical, worldly patriarch's trust in a disembodied voice. This is becoming, however incredibly, the story of an interpersonal relationship.

Sarai the pawn, however, has not been let in on any of this and grumbles against a god "who has obstructed me from bearing," even after ten years in Canaan. Faithful to the customs of her time, she presents Avram with her Egyptian maid as sexual surrogate, so that "perhaps I may be built-up-with-sons through her!" But once the maid, Hagar, becomes pregnant, she begins to treat her mistress dismissively, which is more than poor Sarai can take. When Avram gives Sarai leave to treat Hagar as she will, Sarai's beatings drive Hagar out of the encampment into the wilderness, where an angel instructs her to return to Sarai, no matter the abuse, for Hagar too will have seed "too many to count." Her son Yishmael (or Ishmael) shall be another Enkidu, "a wild-ass of a man, his hand against all, hand of all against him"—father of the Arabs. Distraught Hagar does as she is bid, but not before giving a new name to the god whose presence is signaled by the angelic messenger. She calls him "God of Seeing" and "the Living-One Who-Sees-Me," and it is just this Seeing that will occupy the rest of the narrative.

Avram is now a very old man—according to our text, ninety-nine. And though we may take this number as a faint echo of Sumerian exaggeration, there is no reason to doubt that Avram and Sarai are well beyond the hope of children of their bodies. But the god is becoming more than a voice: he is "seen" by Avram, who is told, "I am God Shaddai"—a name for which we may have lost the linguistic key, though many have thought it means "Mountain God" or "God of the High Place." "Walk in my presence!" invites the god. "And be wholehearted!" Seeing the god in all his splendor and being invited to such intimacy causes Avram to fall "upon his face." The relationship is becoming more intense; and as we witness its development, we must acknowledge something just below the surface of events: without Avram's highly colored sense of himself—of his own individuality—there could hardly be any relationship, yet the relationship is also made possible by the exclusive intensity that this incipient monotheism requires, so much so that we may almost say that individuality (with its consequent possibility of an inter-personal relationship) is the flip side of monotheism.

Once again, the god promises Avram the land of Canaan and progeny beyond all telling, even royal progeny ("yes, kings will go out from you"). And now the god wants to covenant with Avram, just as chieftains covenant with one another. In this covenant, Avram is to have a new name, Avraham (or Father-of-Many-Nations), as is Sarai, who will henceforth be Sara (or Princess). Avram and his god are to establish an unbreakable bond, which in this period was al-ways contracted in blood, usually the blood of animal sacri-fice. But the blood of this covenant is to be Avram's own and that of "every male among you":

> "At eight days old, every male among you shall be
>   circumcised, throughout your generations,
> whether house-born or bought with money from any
>   foreigner, who is not your seed.
> Circumcised, yes, circumcised shall be your house-born and
>   your money-bought (slaves),
> so that my covenant may be in your flesh as a covenant for
>   the ages."

It is impossible for any man to forget his penis, his own personal life force. By this covenant, the children of Avram will be virtually unable to forget the god who never forgets them and who in his growing splendor and exclusivity appears less and less like a portable amulet to be rubbed for good luck. This god is losing the guardian-angel aspect of the Sumerian patronal gods and is turning into—God. To us this covenant may appear barbaric. But within the rigid simplicities of Canaan and Mesopotamia, this "covenant in your flesh," this permanent reminder, makes perfect sense.

The man who is now Avraham, still on his face, begins to laugh, thinking, "To a hundred-year-old-man shall there be (children) born? Or shall ninety-year-old Sara give birth?" Then aloud: "If only Yishmael might live in your presence!"—in other words, let the promise fall to Yishmael, who has the great virtue of already existing. Avraham is only trying to help God out, get him to be more realistic. But though God will make Yishmael bear fruit "exceedingly, exceedingly," his covenant shall be with the child "whom Sara will bear you at this set-time, another year hence." So Sara the pawn, who's never gotten anything she wants out of life, is to become pregnant in three months. At last, something tangible.

"When he had finished speaking with Avraham, God went up, from beside Avraham." Interview over; circumcisions begin. And barely has Avraham finished circumcising himself and "all his household" than visitors arrive. Avraham, no doubt a little winded from his activity, is "sitting at the entrance to his tent at the heat of the day"—just as we can see Bedouin chieftains in the punishing sun of today's Middle East, sitting under their tent flap, hoping to catch a breeze.

He lifted up his eyes and saw:

here, three men standing over against him.

When he saw them, he ran to meet them from the entrance
    to his tent and bowed to the earth

and said:

"My lords,

pray if I have found favor in your eyes,

pray do not pass by your servant!

Pray let a little water be fetched, then wash your feet and
    recline under the tree;

let me fetch (you) a bit of bread, that you may refresh your
    hearts,

then afterward you may pass on—

for you have, after all, passed your servant's way!"

Avraham, however well established in his herds and retainers, thinks himself well below the mark of these "lords,"
whoever they may be, and is eager to demonstrate to them
his surpassing hospitality. What he has in mind is considerably more than "a bit of bread." Running to Sara and shout-
ing "make haste!" he commands her to bake three cakes
from their best semolina. Then he's off to the oxen to choose
a calf, "tender and fine," for a servant to prepare. When the
meal is ready, Avraham himself serves it with solicitude.
While the potentates eat, they ask after his wife, whose name
they somehow know:

"Where is Sara your wife?"

"Here in the tent," replies Avraham with mounting sus-
picion.

The lord sitting in the middle of the three says:

"I will return, yes, return to you when time revives [that is, a year from now] and Sara your wife will have a son."

Avraham knows now that he is entertaining God and two angels,* but Sara, who knows nothing of the previous promises (why would a man share such things with a wife?), has overheard. Perhaps she is giddy from all her frantic baking, but she finds the conversation ludicrous and chuckles to herself, "After I have become worn, is there to be pleasure for me? And my lord is *old!*"

"Now why does Sara laugh?" asks the figure in the middle, who now reveals himself as the God for whom no feat is impossible, and repeats the promise. Poor Sara, full of fear and confusion, insists she did not laugh. "No," says God, "indeed you laughed." Sara, who has been left out of the great relationship between her husband and God, laughs the laugh of the ancient world, of Sumer, Egypt, and Canaan, of Europe, Asia, Australia, and the Americas, the rightly cynical laugh of all those who know that a woman cannot bear children past menopause and a man cannot get it up in advanced old age. For all the tall tales of heroes and kings, the world of human experience is as predictable as the zodiac that turns in the heavens. We all know the final inevitability, how things must end.

This episode blends effortlessly into the next. God debates within himself whether he will tell Avraham "what I am about

* At this early period, angels, another borrowing from the Sumerians, are seen as manifestations of God, often hardly distinguishable from him. This scene of the three heavenly visitors breaking bread before Avraham's tent is the subject of Andrei Rublev's painting, the greatest of all Russian icons.

to do" and decides to speak privately with Avraham because "I have known him"—while the two angels head for Sodom, where Lot lives. When God reveals his plan of destruction for Sodom and Gomorrah, Avraham attempts to reason with him: "Will you really sweep away the innocent along with the guilty?" By questioning God, who has been gradually revealing his awesome grandeur to Avraham, the patriarch exhibits striking courage, a courage that will reappear in his descendants throughout the ages to come. A verbal tug-of-war ensues, ending with God's promise to stay his hand if as few as ten innocents are found within the walls of these cities.

Fade-in: Sodom's main square, where Lot, encountering the angels, invites them to stay at his house. (Though not as generous to his guests as Avraham, he's undoubtedly a good guy.) But the men of the city surround the house like the ghouls in *Night of the Living Dead* and demand that Lot bring out the two handsome young men so they can, well, sodomize them. It becomes all too clear that there aren't ten innocents here. There's only Lot, who tries to buy time with a ploy that might not have occurred to most of us in his situation:

Now pray, I have two daughters who have never known a
   man,
pray let me bring them out to you, and you may deal with
   them however seems good in your eyes;
only to these men do nothing,

for they have, after all, come under the shadow of my roof
beam!

Of course, the Sodomites aren't interested and roar that
they will bugger Lot, too, once they have broken down the
door. But no one gets buggered; and the Sodomites get
theirs—fire and brimstone from heaven—once Lot and his
family are out of the way, save, unfortunately, for Lot's wife,
who looks back on the raining destruction, even though she
has been told not to, and gets turned into a pillar of salt—
another wifely pawn.

This unhappy episode, beloved of sexually repressed fundamentalists through the ages, may leave most of us with the
same reaction Evelyn Waugh described one of his fellow
officers as having. The young man, an empty-headed dilet-
tante right out of the pages of Wodehouse, had never read
anything, but during the longeurs between military engage-
ments he decided to while away the hours by reading a book
for the very first time, and the Bible was all that was available. Having read part of Genesis, he soon gave up the pursuit, exclaiming: "God, what a shit God is!"

It is only somewhat mollifying to realize that the sin of
Sodom was not homosexuality but inhospitality. You can't
tell from this episode whether God is against buggery, but
you can be sure he takes a dim view of raping perfectly nice
strangers who come to visit. Also, we know from widespread
Mesopotamian evidence that Sumerians and other ancient
peoples of the Middle East preferred rear entry, both vaginal

and anal, for their sexual encounters. To the descendants of Avraham, who viewed such posture as subhuman ("like a dog"), the whole sexual repertoire of their neighbors may have come to seem suspect—bestial and unnatural.

But now we go from the fire and brimstone to a real wonder:

Sara became pregnant and bore Avraham a son in his old
  age,
at the set-time of which God had spoken to him.
And Avraham called the name of his son, who was born to
  him, whom Sara bore to him:
Yitzhak (He Laughs) [Isaac in traditional English translation].
And Avraham circumcised Yitzhak his son at eight days old,
  as God had commanded him. . . .
Now Sara said:
"God has made me laugh."

God had made her laugh before—by suggesting the impossible. Now Sara the pawn is given the only thing she ever wanted, the very thing she knew she could not have. She wanted this child much more than Avraham did—however keen his desire had been—for he could have children by other women. It is one of the hallmarks of the handiwork of Avraham's God that his purpose for one human being spills over into the lives of others, creating bliss even for the story's supernumeraries. The conversation between these two (who have barely conversed before, at least in our presence) is rich and poignant, and the speech of her who has hardly spoken has a pathos such as we would expect only from a great writer of dialogue:

"God has made me laugh,
all who hear of it will laugh for me. . . .
Who would have declared to Avraham:
'Sara will nurse sons?'
Well, I have borne him a son in his old age!"

God has made Avraham laugh, God has made Sara laugh, God makes Yitzhak laugh. And: "The child grew and was weaned, and Avraham made a great drinking-feast on the day that Yitzhak was weaned." At this point, winter has been dispelled and everyone's nightmares are over.

Not quite.
For one thing, Sara is determined that Hagar the Egyptian will not share in the laughter and drives out her and her son for good (though they remain under God's protection). And then, in piercing staccato phrases, the narrator begins the Hebrew Bible's most fearful and piteous story:

Now after these events it was
that God tested Avraham
and said to him
"Avraham!"
He said:
"Here I am."

He said:

"Pray take your son,

your only-one,

whom you love,

Yitzhak,

and go-you-forth to the land of Moriyya (Seeing),

and offer him up there as an offering-up

upon one of the mountains

that I will tell you of."

Avraham started-early in the morning,

he saddled his donkey,

he took his two serving-lads with him and Yitzhak his son,

he split wood for the offering-up

and arose and went to the place that God had told him of.

On the third day Avraham lifted up his eyes

and saw the place from afar.

Avraham said to his lads:

"You stay here with the donkey,

and I and the lad will go yonder,

we will bow down and then return to you."

Avraham took the wood for the offering-up,

he placed them upon Yitzhak his son,

in his hand he took the fire and the knife.

Thus the two of them went together.

Yitzhak said to Avraham his father, he said:

"Father!"

He said:

"Here I am, my son."

He said:

"Here are the fire and the wood,
but where is the lamb for the offering-up?"
Avraham said:
"God will see-for-himself to the lamb for the offering-up,
my son."
Thus the two of them went together.
They came to the place that God had told him of;
there Avraham built the slaughter-site
and arranged the wood
and bound Yitzhak his son
and placed him on the slaughter-site atop the wood.
Avraham stretched out his hand,
he took the knife to slay his son.
But [God's] messenger called to him from heaven
and said:
"Avraham! Avraham!"
He said:
"Here I am."
He said:
"Do not stretch out your hand against the lad,
do not do anything to him!
For now I know
that you are in awe of God—
you have not withheld your son, your only-one, from me."
Avraham lifted up his eyes and saw:
there, a ram caught in the thicket by its horns!
Avraham went, he took the ram
and offered it up as an offering-up in the place of his son.
Avraham called the name of that place: [God] Sees.

As the saying is today: On [God's] mountain (it) is seen.

Now [God's] messenger called to Avraham a second time
   from heaven

and said:

"By myself I swear"

—[God's] utterance—

"indeed, because you have done this thing, have not
   withheld your son, your only-one,

indeed, I will bless you, bless you,

I will make your seed many, yes, many,

like the stars of the heavens and like the sand that is on the
   shore of the sea;

your seed shall inherit the gate of their enemies,

all the nations of the earth shall enjoy blessing through your
   seed,

in consequence of your hearkening to my voice."

I doubt anyone has ever read this story, either in the original or in any of its many translations, without being transfixed. Many who heard the story as children and know perfectly well how it will end (with tragedy averted at the very last minute) cannot bring themselves to look at it again or consider seriously "the monster god of the Old Testament," as one woman called him with a shudder. And Fox's plain translation, so close to the bald rhythm of the original Hebrew, is stunning in its cumulative effect, like repeated blows or wounds.

Is this God? What are we to make of such a God? Does the primitive period in which the story takes place somehow explain or excuse the torment that God inflicts on the man and the boy? Isn't the boy, like Sara in the Egyptian story and Lot's wife in the destruction of Sodom, just another pawn in God's game?

Yitzhak is a pawn, surely, even though with swift strokes the narrator gives us a real child who asks a real question. As E. A. Spieser remarks, "The father's answer is tender but evasive, and the boy must by now have sensed the truth. The short and simple sentence, 'And the two of them walked on together' ["Thus the two of them went together" in the Fox translation] covers what is perhaps the most poignant and eloquent silence in all literature." Yes, the narrator's skill is great, leaving the reader speechless at the impending horror.

Interpreters of an anthropological bent have tended to see this story as a symbolic renunciation, the dramatization of some unrecoverable moment in prehistory when the proto-Jews gave up the practice of human sacrifice that their neighbors continued to engage in. Thus it was enshrined in their tradition as a reminder of what they must not do. Christians see in Avraham a type of God, willing to give his "only son" Jesus as sacrifice for our sins. Without meaning to imply that these interpretations have no basis, I hasten to point out that both serve as frames, giving us categories to stuff this episode into: they are excuses to distance ourselves from the central brutality, so that we may eventually tuck it away out of sight. But we must stay with this thing: it is the climax of Avraham's story—the Mountain Experience.

It is tempting to hate Avraham for what he does here. We have already seen him as a wily conniver, blithely willing to sacrifice his own wife to prosper himself. And though we can say to ourselves that the standards of the time were different from our own, it is so difficult to let it go at that—just as difficult as when we try to absolve Thomas Jefferson, prophet of human equality and slaveholder. Still, we must compare Avraham not to ourselves but to Gilgamesh and Hammurabi. When we do this, Avraham begins to stand out from his time in bold relief. However we may loathe Avraham's attitude toward Sara, we cannot doubt that he loves Yitzhak. Indeed, the first time the Bible uses the word *love* is in this very episode:

> Pray take your son,
> your only-one,
> whom you love,
> Yitzhak . . .

It is precisely Avraham's love that makes the episode so unbearable.

The key to this awesome puzzle must lie not in Avraham's relationship to Yitzhak but in his relationship to God. Avraham was a man of Sumer. Initially, "the god" was for Avram little more than Lugalbanda's statue was for Gilgamesh, almost a good luck charm—though from the first there is no statue, no visual manifestation. Even in the earliest stages, then, this relationship is different from the relationships of other Sumerians to their patronal gods. But if the relationship is to last, Avraham requires education; and this he receives in a series of manifestations in which "the god" gradually reveals himself as God—not just a divinity but the only God that counts. We can be certain that Avraham began, like all Sumerians, like all human beings before him (and virtually all after him), as a polytheist, a believer in many (and conflicting) gods and godlets—bad-tempered forces of nature and the cosmos who could be temporarily appeased by just the right rites and rigmarole. It is highly unlikely that Avraham became during the course of his life a strict monotheist, but what we can say is that Avraham's relationship to God became the matrix of his life, the great shaping experience. From voice to vision to august potentate, Avraham's understanding of God grew ever larger; but given the society out of which he came, this understanding remained—by our standards—a very earth-bound one. Something must, after all these years of prepara-tion, jolt him into a recognition of Just-Who-Is-Speaking-to-Him. For the God who calls Avraham to the Mountain Experience must no longer be seen merely as the "Mountain God." He is the opposite of the Sumerian gods with their patently human motivations. He is the God beyond the mountain, even beyond the sky, the unknowable God, whose purposes are hidden from human intelligence, who cannot be manipulated.

And who are we? We are the contingent ones, dependent utterly on this God. And who is Avraham? He is the contin-gent one who must *understand* that he is utterly dependent, who must cling consciously to his God, who gives and takes beyond all understanding. For, as the sage Job will say in later times, "The Lord gives and the Lord takes away: Blessed be the Name of the Lord!"

At the outset of this harrowing episode, the narrator, knowing that poor human readers could never bear the suspense, tells us that this will be a "test," so we know that Yitzhak will not actually be sacrificed, however difficult it is to keep that in mind during the ensuing action. It is a test for us as well. Can we open ourselves to the God who cannot be understood, who is beyond all our amulets and scheming, the God who rains on picnics, the God who allows human beings to be inhuman, who has sentenced us all to death? All the other gods are figments, sorry projections of human desires. Only this God is worth my life (and yours and Yitzhak's). For "there is no other." Avraham must come to believe in a God as awesomely powerful—as Other—as the One whose terrifying presence William Blake, one of Avraham's many inheritors, would one day attempt to invoke:

Tiger, Tiger, burning bright
In the forests of the night,
What immortal hand or eye
Could frame thy fearful symmetry?

Avraham passes the test. His faith—his belief in God—is stronger than his fear. But now he knows he is dealing with the Unthinkable, beyond all expectation. The God who called him out into the wilderness and made impossible promises has begun to bring those promises to fulfillment. But this must not mean that, through this God, I can see the future and control what has not yet come to be. I control nothing. My task is to be as open to God as I am to my own child; to both I must say, "Here I am!"

"Be not afraid," counsels God to Avraham. Be not afraid of his presence in your life. But, paradoxically, be afraid of God's inexplicable omnipotence. For fear of this God, as the Psalmist will one day sing, "is the beginning of wisdom." And this unnamed mountain in the land of Seeing is for Avraham the beginning of fear.

Following this resolution, Avraham's story draws quickly to its close. Sara dies in Hebron and Avraham sets about "to lament for Sara and to weep over her." We might interpret his mourning as merely formal, were it not for what happens next. To bury Sara with all the respect that is due her, Avraham buys his first property in Canaan, but only after waging a nerve-shattering negotiation. Avraham is determined to have "the cave of Makhpela" as Sara's burial chamber. But "a sojourner," even if he were a nomadic chieftain, could not easily buy property in ancient Canaan, and even if he were to convince some stubborn farmer to sell a part of his holdings, the transaction would still be illegal without the consent of the local board of selectmen—in this case the "Sons of Het." The owner of the cave says, with feigned generosity, that since Avraham is so highly respected—"one exalted by God in our midst"—he wouldn't dream of charging him, he can have "the choicest" site free of charge, even the cave of Makhpela, even though it *is* worth four hundred shekels. Avraham hears this and understands what is really being offered: a temporary burial site (with no assurances for the future) for free or a permanent burial site for an outrageous sum. Through all the subsequent bargaining (interminable, full of ritualistic bowing, scraping, and protestations of sincerity, as is still typical of the Middle East), he keeps offering four hundred shekels until it is accepted by all. The amount, probably ten times the cave's actual value, is worth it to Avraham, for it gives him clear and irrevocable title to his wife's final resting place. One feels Avraham would have paid anything for this peace; and thus does he show belatedly, pathetically, his reverence for the matriarch.

It is not long before Avraham joins Sara in the Hebron cave, still contentiously, sometimes tragically, sacred to Arabs and Jews, the grave of the progenitor of both Yishmael and Yitzhak and all their descendants. Avraham does not die before setting in motion an arranged marriage for Yitzhak, a colorless figure of whom we never hear much on his own account—but then think of the poor man's childhood trauma! The stories that follow take us through the lives of the subsequent patriarchs—and matriarchs, since Rivka (or Rebecca), Yitzhak's lively and opinionated wife (who's also a terrific cook and a conniver worthy of her father-in-law), looms especially large in these stories. To Yitzhak, who "loved her" and whom she "comforted after his mother," she bears twin boys, Esav and Yaakov (the traditional Esau and Jacob). When her sons are grown, she conspires with wily Yaakov, her favorite and second-born, to rob loyal Esav of his birthright, by having smooth-skinned Yaakov disguise himself as hairy Esav and present the now-blind Yitzhak with his favorite dish (which she has prepared). The confused old Yitzhak confers on Yaakov the blessing of the firstborn, so that Yaakov succeeds to the line of Avraham and the promises made to him. Despite the pain that this reversal causes Yitzhak, Rivka's plan, as it turns out, is also God's; and throughout Yaakov's life God speaks to him at crucial junctures, not least in the unsettling episode in which a mysterious stranger appears at Yaakov's encampment and wrestles with him all through the night, only to reveal himself in the morning as God and rename Yaakov Yisrael (or Israel), whose children will bear the Promise. Yaakov himself gives God a new name, calling him, for good reason, "the Terror of Yitzhak."

Yaakov/Israel is not the last of the patriarchal figures, but he is the last one to whom God speaks, indeed so intimately that he wrestles: "For I have seen God," exclaims Israel, "face to face—and my life has been saved." To see the face of God and live: this will be for the Children of Israel in all their subsequent generations the unreachable acme of holiness. The first stage of the Promise has been fulfilled, and both Avraham and Israel have "walked with God." The religious center is no longer what it had been for the Sumerians and all other ancient cultures—impersonal manipulation by means of ritual prescriptions—but a face-to-face friendship with God. The new religion has been given shape through three generations of nomadic men and women who have ceased to bow down before idols or kings or any earthly image. They have learned, with many fits and starts, to depend on God—and no one else—this inscrutable, terrifying wilderness God.

But no one could maintain such pitch of feeling forever. Now that their consciousness has been altered, there must be a return to the business of ordinary life. No one will walk with God again. No one will see his face or even hear his voice for hundreds of years.

THREE

EGYPT

✴

From Slavery to Freedom

Despite the radical break, there is much continuity between the old world of the Wheel and Avraham's new world of the Journey. Avraham does not turn overnight into a wide-eyed desert mystic, seeking only the Lord. He seeks the things all sane men seek—pleasure and security—though he hopes for something more, something New. And the only immortality sensible Avraham hopes for is heirs of his body. But this is a great deal more than the generalized fertility of Sumer, where sacred prostitutes of both sexes haunted the temple precincts and dead bodies floated along the Euphrates, just as they still do along the Ganges. From now on, the heirs of Avraham will look not to sacred copulation rites but to their God to assure their line and their land.

This God is the initiator: he encounters them; they do not encounter him. He begins the dialogue, and he will see it through. This God is profoundly different from them, not their projection or their pet, not the usual mythological creature whose intentions can be read in auguries or who can be controlled by human rituals. This God gives and takes beyond human reasoning or justification. Because his motives are not interpretable and his thoughts and actions are not foreseeable, anything—and everything—is possible. Many new things have already come into being as a result of this relationship, but faith most of all, which prior to Avraham had no place in religious feeling and imagination. Because all is possible, faith is possible, even necessary.

Despite the fact that Avraham, on reaching Canaan, built an altar at Shekhem, it is true to say that at a deeper level all the sacred places of the world and all its sacred symbols have been cast away. Now everything is sacred, everything profane. Avraham and his children do not anoint special statues or follow the stars from their glistening temples but listen to the Voice and journey on. Faith supplants the generalized predictability of the ancient world with the possibility of both real success and real failure, real happiness and real tragedy—that is, a real journey whose outcome is not yet. Avraham's story is real history and irreversible, not the earthly dramatization of a heavenly exemplar. "Avram went"—really went. Cyclical religion goes nowhere because, within its comprehension, there is no future as we have come to understand it, only the next revolution of the Wheel.

Since time is no longer cyclical but one-way and irreversible, personal history is now possible and an individual life can have value. This new value is at first hardly understood; but already in the earliest accounts of Avraham and his family we come upon the carefully composed genealogies of ordinary people, something it would never have occurred to Sumerians to write down, because they accorded no importance to individual memories. For them only impersonal survival, like the kingship, like the harvest, mattered; the individual, the unusual, the singular, the bizarre—persons or events that did not conform to an archetype—could have no meaning. And without the individual, neither time nor history is possible. But the God of Avraham, Yitzhak, and Yaakov—no longer your typical ancient divinity, no longer the archetypal gesturer—is a real personality who has intervened in real history, changing its course and robbing it of predictability.

He will continue to intervene. And these interventions will gradually bring about in Avraham's descendants enormous changes of mind and heart, some of which are only hinted at in the patriarchal narratives. To give but one example: Yaakov, whose anxious guilt in regard to his brother Esav impels him to expect to be slaughtered at Esav's hands should they ever meet again, at last reconciles with his brother; and in this moment of happy resolution, Yaakov, who has seen the face of God and lived, speaks the uncanny words "Just to see your face is like seeing the face of God, now that you have received me so kindly." The narrator, as is his custom, gives us no help in interpreting this gnomic expression. But we know that in this ancient world to "see the face" of someone was to know him, to understand his character, to grasp his identity. Because Yaakov has seen the face of God—has been allowed, however partially, to know God as he really is, to see into the face of ultimate truth—he can also see an individual human being for who he is; and somehow this experience is like the experience of God. What this will mean for the future is yet to be spelled out, but the human being as pawn (Sara, Lot's daughters, Lot's wife, Yitzhak) is quietly and subtly giving way to a more exalted vision of what a human being is. At this point in the narrative, we have only the faintest hint of such a development. But as we follow the wanderings of Avraham's children down the centuries, we will witness many such developments. We will be witnesses, in fact, to the slow evolution of our entire system of values.

The stories of the patriarchs do not come to their close with the story of Yaakov/Israel. Israel eventually has—by his two wives and two concubines—twelve sons, who are slated to turn into the Twelve Tribes of Israel.* His favorite wife, Rachel, gives him his favorite son, Joseph, the last of the patriarchal figures and the one by whom events are set in motion that bring the Israelites not to permanent settlement in the Promised Land, as might have been expected, but to seemingly permanent slavery in Egypt.

Joseph's brothers, who are wildly jealous of their father's attentions to their youngest half-brother, contrive to sell Joseph to a caravan of slave traders who are passing through Canaan and who take him off to Egypt, where he is bound to a householder named Potiphar. By resisting the sexual attentions of Potiphar's wife, Joseph lands himself in prison, where he gains a reputation for being able to read dreams among the prisoners, one of whom is Pharaoh's cupbearer. When the cupbearer is reprieved and regains his status

---

* The names of the progenitors of the Twelve Tribes (and, subsequently, the names of the tribes themselves) are recorded in Genesis as Reuben, Simeon, Levi, Judah, Issachar, and Zebulun (from Israel's wife Leah); Joseph and Benjamin, the last of Israel's sons (from Israel's wife Rachel); Dan and Naphtali (from the concubine Bilhah); and Gad and Asher (from the concubine Zilpah). In later listings, the tribe of Simeon tends to disappear within the land controlled by Judah; the priestly tribe of Levi, which was landless, is sometimes omitted; and Joseph is divided into the tribes of his sons Ephraim and Manasseh.

in Pharaoh's house, he is able to recommend Joseph as an infallible interpreter of dreams to his master, who has been troubled in his sleep. Joseph's interpretation of Pharaoh's dreams (which, according to Joseph, predict seven years of plenty followed by seven years of famine) so impress Pharaoh as to win Joseph the most extraordinary status—vizier and second-in-command of all Egypt.

In his new position, Joseph sets about to prepare Pharaoh's kingdom for the day of famine by storing much of the grain of plenty. By the time famine strikes, Joseph's stock with Pharaoh and his reputation throughout Egypt could hardly be higher; and it is at this point that Joseph's brothers arrive, impelled by the famine, which has become universal. The Joseph story—a great short story, especially for any reader who has ever been stalked by sibling rivalry—ends with the most satisfying irony: Joseph's brothers are reconciled to him, but not before they have been thoroughly humiliated and made to see that he is their unchallengeable superior; father Yaakov resettles with his family in Egypt, where, surrounded by many grandchildren, he dies happy, extending a special blessing to Joseph's Egyptian children.

Joseph nevers hears the Voice of God, as did his progenitors, the first three patriarchs. But as with the narrative of Rivka's trickery, we are given to understand that all is taking place according to God's will. Just as Yitzhak's torment over giving his blessing to the "wrong" son was a necessary suffering (because it ensured God's will for Avraham's line, which ordinary human thinking would have thwarted), Joseph's suffering at the hands of his brothers and his subsequent slavery were necessary to the eventual survival of the Children of Avraham in famine times. "It was to save life," Joseph explains to his brothers, "that God sent me on before you." This God can make use of human beings, whether they mean to do his will or not.

The Bible now falls silent in its recounting of the story of the generations of Avraham. By the time it picks up the narrative—in Exodus, the second book—centuries have elapsed.* The Children of Israel "bore fruit, they swarmed, they became many, they grew mighty (in number)—exceedingly, yes, exceedingly; the land filled up with them." And then "a new king arose over Egypt," who in the chilling phrase of the King James version "knew not Joseph"—the third pharaoh we encounter in the biblical narrative.

The first pharaoh was a fool—the stationary god-king whom Avram ran circles around. The second, Joseph's pharaoh, is given fairly high marks for a pharaoh: he was smart enough to put Joseph in charge. It is all too likely that this pharaoh was an interloper and a Semite, one of the Hyksos, who ruled Egypt from the time of Hammurabi in the eighteenth century B.C. to the middle of the fourteenth century of the same era, at which time the old royal lines of Egypt reasserted themselves. One of these post-Hyksos pharaohs was Akhnaton, who for a brief period decreed that only one god,

* How many centuries is debatable. For the approximate dates of the principal events of the Hebrew Bible, see the chronology at the back of the book. For an annotated table of contents of the Hebrew Bible, see "The Books of the Hebrew Bible," also at the back.

Aton the Solar Disc, could be worshiped publicly in Egypt. But this singular reform was carried out in the teeth of vested interests (the priests and votaries of all the other gods) and was soon rescinded by a subsequent pharaoh, the mighty Tutankhamon, and erased from public memory. The pharaoh who "knew not Joseph" was most probably Seti I, who reached the throne of Egypt thirty-four years after Tutankhamon and more than a half-century after Akhnaton.

This pharaoh (he is never given a proper name in the Bible, as if the writer would not give him even that much dignity) is beset by a fear so great we would call it paranoia: he fears that there are now so many "Children of Israel" that they may even be "many-more and mightier (in number) than we"—a sure sign of paranoia, since the Israelites could hardly have become that numerous—and that "if war should occur," this people may also "be added to our enemies and make war upon us or go away from the land!" His solution: to impress the Israelites into forced labor to build his great storage cities of Pitom and Rameses.

Still fearing their numbers, he attempts to enlist their midwives in a feeble attempt at genocide—the first but hardly the last that the Children of Israel will endure. He summons two women who are termed "the midwives of the Hebrews." In contrast to his impersonal treatment of Pharaoh, the god-king of all Egypt, the narrator records the names of these humble women: Shifra and Pua. Their very names seem to call them up from the distant past; and we can almost see them standing before Pharaoh, the young, beautiful one with the young, beautiful name, the old, plain one with the old, plain name, listening to him rave:

"When you help the Hebrew women give birth, look at the two stones:
if it is a boy, kill him;
but if a girl, let her live."

It has been objected that this scene could not possibly be historical: if you want to kill off a people, you must assassinate their women, their baby factories, not their men. What Pharaoh urges is irrational on two levels: he is trying to destroy his own labor force—and he is going about it inefficiently. Nor could two midwives do the whole job if Israel had become so numerous.

But what about those "two stones"? They could (as some commentators have thought) be something on the order of medieval birthing stools, but why more than one? The Bible often employs euphemism in describing sexual (especially male) anatomy. To me, the meaning leaps out: the minute the midwife sees that the newborn has testicles, she is to smother him.

And why must we think of Pharaoh as rational? Have we not already been given the evidence that he is irrational— that he thinks the Children of Israel are "many-more and mightier" than the Egyptians? Is it perhaps only in Pharaoh's eyes that the Children of Israel "swarm," as if they were breeding insects? Is this a weak, fantasy-beset god-king who fears the potency of the Israelites, much as enervated plantation owners of the American South feared the potency of their black slaves, especially those slaves who had "two stones"? Would the Nazi attempt to destroy the Children of Israel be any more rational than this (less efficient) one? I do not doubt that what we have here is the portrayal—in a few deft strokes—of an insecure Egyptian madman, an all-powerful god-king who fears that someone else could be more powerful than he.

"But," continues the narrator in his usual economic fashion,

> the midwives held God in awe,
> and they did not do as the king of Egypt had spoken to
>   them,
> they let the children live.

Such beautiful, simple words. Because they bowed down before real power, they were not tempted to bow down before empty show, and so they did the right thing. It is less than clear that these "midwives of the Hebrews" were themselves Children of the Promise; they may have been pagans who bore the true God in their hearts, they may have been, like Hagar, Egyptians who could See. But in their exquisite moral discernment ("they let the children live") they are people of stature—real individuals who are worthy of names, unlike the little god-king. Nor should we forget that they are women, who in their sharp insight into the deep truth of things have taken a giant evolutionary step beyond Sara the pawn, beyond Avraham himself, who was willing to sacrifice his wife to save his own neck.

The next turn of the screw is even more satisfying. When Pharaoh learns that the midwives have disobeyed him, he summons them once more with a petulant "Why have you done this thing?"

> The midwives said to Pharaoh:
> "Indeed, not like the Egyptian (women) are the Hebrew (women),
> indeed they are lively:
> before the midwife comes to them, they have given birth!"

Once again, we are back on that southern plantation, where well-brought-up "ladies" need potions and medical assistance just to keep from fainting on a hot day, but slave women are so full of life that they drop their young with as little ado as barnyard animals—and the oppressed subvert the overlord with seeming guilelessness.

The exasperated god-king takes a further step into irrationality and orders that henceforth all newborn Hebrew males be thrown into the Nile. Thus it is that we are introduced to a Hebrew mother, a woman who

> became pregnant and bore a son.
> When she saw him—that he was goodly, she hid him, for three months.
> And when she was no longer able to hide him,
> she took for him a little-ark of papyrus,
> she loamed it with loam and with pitch,

placed the child in it,
and placed it in the reeds by the shore of the Nile.
Now his sister stationed herself far off, to know what would
    be done to him.

This lovely passage, full of care and cherishing—how seldom the narrator allows himself to rest in such humble details as loam and pitch—presents us with a loving mother and a loving sister, who also exhibit the characteristic resourcefulness we have come to expect of the Children of Abraham. The rest of the episode is so well known that I need only summarize it: Pharaoh's daughter, one of the long line of biblical figures who See, spots the little-ark among the bullrushes while bathing in the Nile, sees the child, and takes pity on him, though she knows perfectly well that he is "one of the Hebrews' children." The baby's sister suddenly materializes and helpfully volunteers to find for the princess a nursemaid "from the Hebrews"—a nursemaid who turns out to be the baby's mother. Thus is the child rescued from certain death by a silent conspiracy of women on the side of life, so that he can grow up as an Egyptian prince with a secret Jewish* mother, a man who will understand the world of power and connections, but a man who has also been nursed at the breasts of kindness and love—the best of both worlds. The princess gives him the name Moshe (or Moses), He-Who-Pulls-Out.

* "Jewish" is a conscious anachronism on my part. The people who would become the Jews were known in this period as Hebrews or (perhaps) Hapiru—that is, the "Dusty Ones" from the mountains and deserts. To themselves they were the Children of Israel.

This is all we need to know about Moshe's childhood—and in the next scene Moshe, the grown man, does exactly what we would expect of him: "he went out to his brothers and saw their burdens." The lovingly nurtured prince identifies with the underdog; and seeing an Egyptian repeatedly strike one of his brothers, he kills the Egyptian and buries him in the sand. The following day, in a scene that foreshadows the great anguish of Moshe's future life—the carping opposition of his own "stiffnecked" people—he breaks up a scuffle between two Hebrews, only to have the guilty party taunt him:

"Who made you prince and judge over us?
Do you mean to kill me
as you killed the Egyptian?"

So "the matter is known"; and hard on the heels of this gossip, Pharaoh seeks to execute Moshe for his crime, leaving Moshe no alternative but flight.

Moshe finds refuge in the land of Midian, where he is given shelter and a shepherd's occupation by Jethro, whose daughter Tzippora Moshe marries. Their first child Moshe names Gershom, aptly meaning Sojourner There, "for he said," as the King James has it, "I have been a stranger in a strange land." And this strange land is about to yield up to this stranger the strangest experience ever known.

Moshe, shepherding Jethro's flock, leads the sheep "behind the wilderness" to a mountain called Horeb, another name for Sinai. The text signals to us that something extraordinary is about to happen by calling this place "the mountain of God," but there is no reason to suspect that Moshe is anticipating anything more than another energy-sapping day with the flock. Moshe sees, out of the corner of his eye, "the flame of a fire out of the midst of a bush." He stops to take in this unusual sight, for in the desert any movement stands out as phenomenal, and observes that "the bush is burning with fire, and the bush is not consumed!" Even though the dehydrating desert heat is a constant warning to nomadic herders against making any but the most necessary exertions, Moshe resolves to "turn aside that I may see this great sight—why the bush does not burn up!"

As Moshe makes his way toward the fire, God calls "out of the midst of the bush," twice speaking Moshe's name, as he once did to Avraham on the Mountain of Seeing:

"Moshe! Moshe!"
He said:
"Here I am."

—the very words Avraham used.

He said:
"Do not come near to here,
put off your sandal from your foot [just as the Arabs still do
    on holy ground],
for the place on which you stand—it is holy ground!"

And he said:
"I am the God of your father,
the God of Avraham,
the God of Yitzhak,
and the God of Yaakov."

In the midst of this breaking of the silence of hundreds of years—this completely unexpected manifestation of continuity—Moshe, the Egyptian prince who could hardly have been less prepared for such a moment, acts with a terror the patriarchs seldom exhibited:

Moshe concealed his face,
for he was afraid to gaze upon God.

But God reveals that, despite appearances (or lack thereof), he has not been absent:

"I have seen, yes, seen the affliction of my people that is in
    Egypt,
their cry have I heard in the face of their slave-drivers;
indeed I have known their sufferings!
So I have come down
to rescue it from the hand of Egypt,
to bring it up from that land,
to a land, goodly and spacious,
to a land flowing with milk and honey. . . .
So now, go,

for I send you to Pharaoh—
bring my people, the Children of Israel, out of Egypt!"

Here is Moshe, on his face in the intense desert heat, made even fiercer by the fire before him, listening to a Voice that no one has heard since the days of Yaakov, a Voice that orders him off on an impossible mission to the very people he has been hiding from. Like Avraham, he never doubts the information of his senses—that this is really happening—only God's lack of realism:

"Who am I
that I should go to Pharaoh,
that I should bring the Children of Israel out of Egypt?"

God's answer ignores completely Moshe's opinion of himself. For this mission will not be dependent on Moshe's abilities but on God's:

"Indeed, I will be-there with you,
and this is the sign for you that I myself have sent you:
when you have brought the people out of Egypt,
you will (all) serve God by this mountain."

Moshe now offers one objection after another in the vain hope of forestalling God. He imagines confronting the Children of Israel with the news that "the God of your fathers has sent me," only to receive their skeptical response: "They will say to me: 'What is his name?' " Moshe, the clean-shaven ward of Pharaoh with the style and bearing of an Egyptian, will hardly seem a credible messenger of God in the eyes of the dusty slaves, and they will quiz him merci-lessly till they call his bluff.

God's reply is probably the greatest mystery of the Bible. He tells Moshe his name, all right:

"Yhwh."

What does it mean? Ancient Hebrew was written without vowels; and by the time vowel subscripts were added to the consonants in the Middle Ages, the Name of God had be-come so sacred that it was never uttered. Even in classical times, as early as the Second Temple period, only the high priest could pronounce the Name of God—and only once a year in the prayer of the Day of Atonement. Once the Tem-ple was destroyed in A.D. 70, no Jew ever uttered the Name again. From that time to this, the devout have avoided this word in the text of their Bible, reading *"Adonai"* ("the Lord") when they come to the word *Yhwh*. Many Ortho-dox go a step further, refusing even to say *"Adonai"* and substituting *"ha-Shem"* ("the Name"). So, after such a great passage of time, we have lost the certain knowledge of how to pronounce the word that is represented by these conso-nants. And, without the pronunciation, we are less than cer-tain of its meaning, since precise meaning in Hebrew is often dependent on knowing how to pronounce the vowels, especially in the case of verbs—and YHWH is definitely a verb form.

We can take comfort in the certain knowledge that God is a verb, not a noun or adjective. His self-description is not static but active, appropriate to the God of Journeys. YHWH is an archaic form of the verb *to be;* and when all the commentaries are taken into account, there remain but three outstanding possibilities of interpretation, none of them mutually exclusive. First, *I am who am:* this is the interpretation of the Septuagint, the ancient Greek translation of the Hebrew Bible, which because of its age and its links to the ancients bears great authority. It was this translation that Thomas Aquinas used in the thirteenth century to build his theology of God as the only being whose essence is Existence, all other beings being contingent on God, who is Being (or Is-ness) itself. A more precise translation of this idea could be: "I am he who causes (things) to be"—that is, "I am the Creator." Second, *I am who I am*—in other words, "None of your business" or "You cannot control me by invoking my name (and therefore my essence) as if I were one of your household gods." Third, *I will be-there with you:* this is Fox's translation, following Martin Buber and Franz Rosenzweig, which emphasizes God's continuing presence in his creation, his being-there with us.

How should we pronounce the Name when we come upon it? One may, of course, substitute "the Lord" for the tetragrammaton YHWH. Others will boldly attempt a pronunciation, *"Yahweh"* (as English speakers usually say it) or *"Yahvé"* (after the French and Germans) or even "Jehovah" (a mispronunciation, much in evidence in Protestant hymnody and based on an inadequate understanding of the conventions of medieval manuscripts). But for me, when I attempt to say the consonants without resort to vowels, I find myself just breathing in, then out, with emphasis, in which case God becomes the breath of life. This God of the fathers, now manifested as YHWH in the bush that burns but is not consumed, is more awesome than in any of his previous manifestations—not only because of the fireworks, but because of the symbolic nature of this epiphany, which suggests that this God, as dangerous, tempering, and purifying as fire, can burn in us without consuming.

God explains to Moshe how things will go before Pharaoh, who "will not give you leave to go" until God strikes Egypt "with all my wonders"; and he arms Moshe with a few wonders of his own for dazzling the multitude. But then, Moshe raises his most serious objection:

"Please, my Lord,
no man of words am I . . .
for heavy of mouth and heavy of tongue am I!"
YHWH said to him:
"Who placed a mouth in human beings . . . ?
So now, go!
I myself will instruct you as to what you are to speak."

Moshe continues to drag his feet, so that "YHWH's anger flared up against Moshe"—and not for the last time. At last,

God offers the tongue-tied shepherd-prince his brother Aharon (or Aaron) to be Moshe's spokesman: "he shall be for you a mouth, and you, you shall be for him a god." And then "Moshe went." In this long procession of God's delegates through the ages, the pattern established by Avraham holds: they may object vigorously, but then, when all's said and done, they *go*. They remain faithful—full of faith.

But Moshe is still the uncut Egyptian prince, not yet a convenanted son of Israel, so on the journey back to Egypt "YHWH encountered him and sought to make him die"— "to kill him" being the usual translation. Tzippora, in the long tradition of practical wives, intuits immediately what is wrong. "Tzippora took a flint and cut off her son's foreskin, she touched it to" Moshe's—"feet" or "legs" we would normally translate the next word of the text. But once again, ancient Hebrew literature is reticent when it comes to designating genitals, especially male genitals. Tzippora touches her son's foreskin to Moshe's penis and screams: "Indeed, a bridegroom of blood are you to me!"

What a scene this must have been—little Gershom the Sojourner screaming in one corner; blood dripping from Gershom, running down Tzippora's forearms, smeared on Moshe's foreskin; Tzippora's unhinged, triumphant exclamation; the abrupt withdrawal of God's wrath. This is but another story by which all, even those who had taken on the mores of alien societies, could come to understand: the covenant in blood is serious business. And in this ancient religious milieu, still harking back to old ideas of correspondence and the power of blood, to have one's foreskin washed in the blood of one's son's foreskin was to have been circumcised.

This God is obviously not a member of any known "twelve-step program." He is far from "supportive" and "inclusive," to use the jargon of our day—and he is certainly not cuddly. Perhaps he is not a God for an age such as ours but for a more vigorous one, such as the Jacobean, that did not blanch so easily. "Batter my heart," prayed John Donne to this alien God,

> That I may rise, and stand, o'erthrow me, and bend
> Your force, to break, blow, burn and make me new. . . .
> Take me to You, imprison me, for I
> Except You enthrall me, never shall be free,
> Nor ever chaste, except You ravish me.

Following this bloody episode, Moshe, exuding a new-found confidence and with Aharon as his spokesman, succeeds in winning the confidence of "all the elders of the Children of Israel." He then makes his approach to the dread Pharaoh—a new pharaoh, probably Seti's son Rameses II, since the Bible tells us that the pharaoh who enslaved the Israelites had died by the time of Moshe's encounter at the burning bush.

"**W**ho is YHWH?" inquires Pharaoh,

"that I should hearken to his voice to send Israel free?
I do not know YHWH,
moreover, Israel I will not send free!"

These are the first words the new god-king speaks on his first appearance in the Book of Exodus. The words of this question, like the notes of an identifying musical phrase in grand opera, give us the principal "notes" of Pharaoh's character. The question is the key that opens up Pharaoh's soul to public view. But more than this, it is a leitmotif not only for Exodus, but for many of the books that make up the library that we call the Bible—to such an extent that it could almost be said to be the central question posed by these scriptures.

Who is YHWH? However we interpret it, the Name of God means ultimate dominion: He-Whom-There-Is-No-Escaping. This idea must have been implicit in even the earliest form of this narrative concerning the intervention of the Israelite God in human affairs—and it was an idea to which the Israelites, in different ways at different times, became accustomed. So much so that Pharaoh's question must have had for the first audiences to hear the story a satisfyingly ironic ring, even a savagely comical ring, especially satisfying in that its irony was unperceived by this pretentious pipsqueak. Who is YHWH? Pharaoh is about to find out. He is about to have his ears boxed—and only he is unaware of it. So to the audiences who first heard this story told, the phrase "Who is YHWH?" sounded the ominous notes of Pharaoh's doom—just as the famous five-note phrase in Bizet's *Carmen* foreshadows Carmen's violent end.

The narrative of the ten plagues, each plague brought on the Egyptians by Pharaoh's pigheaded refusal to heed YHWH's demand and let the Israelites leave his dominion, is too well known to recount in detail. Each time Moshe and his brother Aharon approach Pharaoh with YHWH's demand, Pharaoh refuses. Though he begins to offer unacceptable, minor concessions, plague follows plague: the Nile reeking with blood, a swarm of frogs (who die and lie in festering heaps), fleas "on man and beast," an infestation of insects, a pestilence that kills livestock, boils, hail, locusts, "darkness over the land," and, last of all, the one that breaks Pharaoh's spirit, the death of the firstborn of Egypt—from "the firstborn of Pharaoh" and of every Egyptian household to "every firstborn of beast."

Why is Pharaoh so obstinate? God predicted he would be ("I am well aware that the king of Egypt will not let you go unless he is compelled by a mighty hand") and even claimed responsibility for Pharaoh's attitude ("but I myself will make him obstinate, and he will not let the people go"). Are we, therefore, to conclude that Pharaoh is just another pawn with no will of his own? Rather, I think, the text suggests strongly that Pharaoh is acting in character—as would any great monarch divinely appointed.

In ancient Egypt, the pharaoh was god-on-earth, the visible manifestation of the presence of Ra, chief god of the Egyptians. But *ra'a* also means "evil" in Hebrew; and if the pharaoh was Rameses II, his name—a combination of *ra* and *moses*—would have sounded to a Hebrew ear like "he who brings forth evil," the evil counterpart of Moses. In the parlance of the ancient world, moreover, the phrase "the hand of god X" was virtually an idiom used to describe a plague, so that we may interpret the phrase "the hand of YHWH," which is repeated throughout the plague narrative, as belonging to this attributional tradition. If plagues were commonly considered divine in origin within Egyptian society, what we have here is an account of a cosmic tug-of-war between two gods—Ra and YHWH—played out on earth between their designated stand-ins—Pharaoh and Moshe. Within this interpretation, YHWH's promise to Moshe "I will make you as a god to Pharaoh" may have even deeper implications than at first appear.

However that may be, Pharaoh's consciousness of his role as the Sun god incarnate, whose epithets include "Son of Ra" and "Good God," would have made him obstinate: his whole worldview is at stake. If he gives in to this upstart YHWH, the consequences are too terrible to contemplate, for these consequences include losing control over the natural order. Pharaoh, as the Son of Ra, is responsible for the orderly functioning of the Nile and the fertility of the land. In the ancient world, chaos, especially chaos in nature, especially the drying up of fertility, was always greatly to be feared—much more feared than it is by us who seem, from our technological point of view, far better protected from such chaos. So when God tells Moshe that he will "make [Pharaoh] obstinate," he is referring to the very nature of things: this is the way things are; they can be no other way.

God understands the nature of things (and of individual human beings) as does no other, for he has created all nature, as he stresses repeatedly in his encounters with his creatures:

> "Who placed a mouth in human beings
> or who (is it that) makes one mute or deaf
> or open-eyed or blind?
> Is it not I, YHWH?"

God knows who Pharaoh is and therefore foresees the inevitability of his obstinacy.

But there is deeper human and theological business at work in this story than the theme of the inevitability of Pharaoh's behavior. God the Creator has ultimate dominion over all he has created; earthly dominion is given to men only in a subsidiary sense—only insofar as they conform their actions to God's will. Pharaoh must fail because he is not so conformed. The god whose representative he is, is powerless before YHWH; he is as nothing, so much so that he never even makes an appearance in the narrative: his residual presence is like the faintest scent, discoverable only by an inquiry into linguistic roots.

The comedy of the narrative lies in ironic juxtaposition: Pharaoh, supposedly all-powerful, understands nothing. It would not be too much to say that this narrative asserts that power (because it is a feckless attempt to usurp God's dominion) makes you stupid, blinding you to your true situation—and absolute power makes you absolutely stupid. The simple audience of semi-nomadic herdsmen to whom this story was first told understood that they were wiser than Pharaoh: they, certainly, unlike the great Ra-Moses, now with frogs jumping all over him, now covered in horseflies, would not have required the cumulative impact of *ten* plagues to change course! And this audience would also have appreciated the paradox that they were also more powerful than Pharaoh, because God is on the side of the little people, the people who have no worldly power. This is a lesson that will be repeated again and again in the story of Israel.

It is precisely Pharaoh's pretense to a dominion that he does not own—the very motivation of his actions throughout the plague narrative—that is mocked in Exodus, that gives the narrative its satirical edge. The lesson is so cunningly shaped as drama—ten separate plagues, any one of which might have convinced a more ordinary mortal to give in—that it burns itself into the memory like a brand: when a human being arrogates to himself the role of God, he must fail miserably.

The implications of this lesson were radical in their time, since there was no political edifice that did not claim to be founded by a god. In one fell swoop, this subversive narrative delegitimizes all political structures claiming a god as their author—delegitimizes, in fact, all the political structures of the ancient world. And Pharaoh, who claimed to know nothing of YHWH, has come to know him all too well, "and there was a great cry in Egypt; for there is not a house in which there is not a dead man."

Like Avram before them, the Children of Israel are sent forth from Egypt richer than they arrived, with "objects of silver and objects of gold, and clothing" that the Egyptians press upon them to encourage them to leave. "So," concludes the narrator compactly, "did they strip Egypt." They also transport with them the "bones of Joseph," the mummy of the forefather. They do not take the obvious route to Canaan—by way of the coast, now occupied by the warrior "sea people," the Philistines—"lest the people regret it, when they see war, and return to Egypt!" God is apparently afraid that this people he has decided to champion have little fortitude and may use any calamity as an excuse to return to the security of their previous servitude.

Their route—by way of the wilderness at the Sea of Reeds (not the "Red Sea," a mistranslation)—is unrecoverable and the source of myriad scholarly disputes. But we should probably imagine this "sea" as more a marsh than a large body of water; and when Pharaoh, in a change of heart, charges after them with all his chariots and charioteers, we should probably imagine the miracle that we know is coming on a somewhat less heroic scale than its usual dramatizations would have it.

As the forces of Egypt march toward them, the Children of Israel turn on Moshe (it doesn't take them long to lose heart), crying:

"Is it because there are no graves in Egypt
that you have taken us out to die in the wilderness?
What is this that you have done to us, bringing us out of
    Egypt?

Is this not the very word that we spoke to you in Egypt,
saying: 'Let us alone, that we may serve Egypt!'
Indeed, better for us serving Egypt
than our dying in the wilderness!"

Thus, in a trice, do they reward Moshe's steadfastness in his
long tug-of-war with the god-king and his courage in over-
coming his own inadequacies. But Moshe keeps his head and
his heart, using God's own injunction:

"Do not be afraid!
Stand fast and see
YHWH's deliverance which he will work for you today,
for as you see Egypt today, you will never see it again for
the ages!"

Moshe, the true leader, obeying God's directive, leads the
Children of Israel through the "sea," probably a marsh at
low tide. When Pharaoh and his forces follow, they are beset
by the rising tide, their wheels get stuck in the mud, and
they find themselves in danger of drowning. It would all be
remembered most gloriously by later generations as a miraculous victory:

But the Children of Israel had gone upon dry-land, through
the midst of the sea,
the waters a wall for them on their right and on their left.

So YHWH delivered Israel on that day from the hand of
  Egypt;
Israel saw Egypt dead by the shore of the sea,
and Israel saw the great hand that YHWH had wrought
  against Egypt,
the people held YHWH in awe,
they trusted in YHWH and in Moshe his servant.

That something extraordinary happened here we should
not doubt—and that it happened quickly and to the permanent astonishment of all. Israel, a ragbag of runaway slaves led
by a tongue-tied prince, has triumphed over all the might of
Egypt. But how many were involved—how many dead, how
many saved—and what was the exact disturbance that created the unexpected victory? These are matters that will
probably be argued till the end of time.

The text contains a lengthy song, supposedly sung by
Moshe and the Children of Israel, that reads like an antiph-
ony of praise from an ancient liturgy. In it, YHWH is depicted
as a warrior god and the greatest of all the gods ("Who is like
you among the gods, O YHWH!"); and Israel is depicted as
"your people redeemed" whom "you led in your faithfulness." This incredible surprise, this permanent victory
wrested from the very jaws of expected disaster and predictable defeat, left a profound impression on the imagination of
the whole people—now no longer merely the Children of
Avraham or of Israel but the People of YHWH—as had no
earlier encounter between God and any of his chosen inter-

locutors. This was *their* God, the God of Surprises, and they were *his* People.

There is also another song, a brief one with which this scene of triumph closes. On the far shore, beyond the grasp of the devastated Egyptians, a barefoot woman with a timbrel begins to dance, and all the women after her "with timbrels and with dancing." It is Miryam, once the young girl who peered through the bullrushes in the hope of guarding her baby brother, now grown to full womanhood and known to her people as "Miryam the prophetess." Her song is simple and pointed, its Hebrew so archaic that it may well come down to us from the very shore on which she danced, the original formulary from which the song of Moshe and all the accompanying narrative would one day be drawn:

"Sing ye to the LORD,
for he hath triumphed gloriously;
the horse and his rider he hath flung into the sea!"

This story of deliverance is the central event of the Hebrew scriptures. In retrospect, we can see that all the wanderings of the forefathers and foremothers and their growing intimacy with God have led up to this moment; and looking down the ages from this shore, we can see that everything that happens subsequently will be referred back to this moment of astonished triumph. In the next chapter we will take up the vexed question of the Bible's historicity—its reliability as a historical document. But for now it is enough to affirm that in this moment Avraham's descendants, this raggle-taggle collection of Dusty Ones, received an identity they have maintained to this day and to remember this barefoot woman, her dark hair having escaped all confinement, singing and dancing on the far shore with prehistoric exuberance.

FOUR

SINAI

✳

From Death to Life

The story of the Exodus—of Israel's escape from Egypt—has been told and retold so many times down the ages in literature, song, and art that it brings us up short to realize that the story does not belong to history proper, but to the prehistoric lore of a minor Semitic tribe that had not yet learned to read and write, a tribe so unimportant that it makes virtually no appearance in the contemporary history of its powerful—and literate—neighbors. When we examine the considerable extant literatures of Mesopotamia and Egypt, we find no obvious mention of the Israelites. If, as the majority of scholars have provisionally concluded, Israel escaped from Egypt in the reign of Rameses II about midway through the thirteenth century B.C., why is there no record of this marvelous defeat in any Egyptian text or inscription? Of course, the defeat may have been so embarrassing to Egypt that, like many great powers, it could not allow itself to record honestly what happened. Alternatively, the story of the drowning of Pharaoh's army may have been inflated over time by Hebrew oral tradition, and what had been a minor skirmish in Egyptian eyes (we know, for instance, that Rameses II died not in a watery grave but in his bed) was eventually puffed up beyond all recognition. Most radically: the Exodus may never have taken place, but may be just a story concocted, like *Gilgamesh,* by nomadic herdsmen in need of an evening's entertainment.

This last hypothesis, though temptingly unambiguous,

can be maintained only by ignoring certain undeniable aspects of the actual text of the Bible. There are real differences—literary differences, differences of tone and taste, but, far more important, differences of substance and approach to material—between *Gilgamesh* and Exodus, and even between *Gilgamesh* and Genesis. The anonymous authors of *Gilgamesh* tell their story in the manner of a myth. There is no attempt to convince us that anything in the story ever took place in historical time. At every point, rather, we are reminded that the action is taking place "once upon a time"—in other words, in that pristine Golden Time outside meaningless earthly time. The story of Gilgamesh, like the gods themselves, belongs to the realm of the stars. It is meant as a model for its hearers, who believed, in any case, that everything important, everything archetypal, happened, had happened, was happening—it is impossible to fix this occurrence clearly in one tense, since it occurs outside time—beyond the earthly realm of unimportant instances. For all the ancients (except the Israelites, the people who would become the Jews), time as we think of it was unreal; the Real was what was heavenly and archetypal. For us, the heirs of Jewish perception, the exact opposite is true: earthly time is real time; Eternity, if we think of it at all, is the end of time (or simply an illusion).

The text of the Bible is full of clues that the authors are attempting to write history of some sort. Of course, as we read the patriarchal narratives of Genesis or the escape-from-Egypt narrative of Exodus, we know we are not reading anything with the specificity of a history of FDR's administration. The people who constructed these narratives did not, like Doris Kearns Goodwin, have access to the card catalogue of the Library of Congress or the resources of the Internet. They had *heard* the story they were writing down, had received it from an oral culture, had in fact received it in two or three variant forms—in the varieties we would expect from tales told over and over down the centuries at one caravan site after another. They did their best to be faithful to their tradition, even if one strand of that tradition occasionally contradicted another. But there is in these tales a kind of specificity—a concreteness of detail, a concern to get things right—that convinces us that the writer has no doubt that each of the main events he chronicles *happened*. More than this, *that* they happened—that God spoke to Avraham and told him to leave Sumer for the unknown, that God spoke to Moshe and told him to lead the Israelites out of Egypt—is the whole point. These are not, like *Gilgamesh,* archetypal tales with a moral at the end: they share nothing essential with other ancient myths from *Gilgamesh* to Aesop to Grimms' fairy tales. If the stories of Cupid and Psyche or Beauty and the Beast never happened in real time, no one is the poorer for that. But if Avraham and Moshe never existed, or if they did not receive their commissions from God, their stories have no point at all—nor does the genetic collection known as "the Jewish people," nor do Christians or Muslims, who also count themselves heirs of Avraham.

We are looking here at one of the great turning points in the history of human sensibility—at an enormous value shift. What was real for the Sumerians (and for all other peoples but the Jews) was the Eternal. What was to become gradually real for the Jews and remains real for us is the here and now and the there and then. The question that springs constantly to our lips—"Did that *really* happen?"—had little meaning in any ancient civilization. For the ancients, nothing new ever did happen, except for the occasional monstrosity. Life on earth followed the course of the stars; and what had been would, in due course, come around again. What was peculiar or unique, like Oedipus's union with his mother, was of necessity monstrous. Surprise was to be eschewed; the wise man looked for the predictable, the repeatable, the archetypal, the eternal. One came to inner peace by coming to terms with the Wheel.

In the two great narratives of the first two books of the Bible, Israel invents not only history but the New as a positive value. It may seem trivial to remark that we could not even have advertising campaigns for soap commercials without the Jews (since soap commercials are always flogging "new" and "revolutionary" improvements). But no "commercial" of the ancient world flogged the New. The beer of the Sumerians was good because of its associations with the eternal, with the archetypal goddess who took care of such things. If the brewer had announced his product as new—as singular and never-before-known—he would have been committing entrepreneurial suicide, for no one would have drunk it. The Israelites, by becoming the first people to live—psychologically—in real time, also became the first people to value the New and to welcome Surprise. In doing this, they radically subverted all other ancient worldviews.

The past is no longer important just because it can be mined for exemplars but because it has brought us to the present: it is the first part of our journey, the journey of our ancestors. So in retelling their life stories, we have a serious obligation to get their histories straight. We are not merely creating literature: we are retelling a personal story that really happened and that has helped to make us the people that we are.

This is what impelled the Israelites to take such care with genealogies—whose son was whom, the names of even such normally unimportant people as wives. And though we cannot expect that the literate redactors—the authors of the Books of Genesis and Exodus, who finally set down this grand jumble of oral material some centuries after the events described—were academic historians, checking and rechecking their facts against the surviving documents of antiquity, we should not doubt that their intention was to write a chronicle of real events, essentially faithful to their sources.

We, reading their work in a wholly different age, surrounded as we are by linguistic and documentary assistance that would have astonished the authors of the Bible, are able to detect many mistakes. We know, for instance, that the name Moshe or Moses, which the authors of Exodus took for a Hebrew name, is actually Egyptian. But this only shows their faithfulness. Though they misguidedly tried to interpret the name as a Hebrew one, they have left us unintentional proof that the man they are writing about was indeed raised as an Egyptian and could have been named by Pharaoh's daughter. This constitutes circumstantial evidence that the story of Moses is true (or at least that he is not a fictional character), for how else could such indirect evidence have been planted in the Bible by authors who could not have meant to put it there? Similarly, the weird incident of the "blood bridegroom," which presents God, the hero of this story, in such a peculiar light, would have been omitted by any author who wished to present a consistent character. It is there only because, however contrary to the image of an all-knowing, all-powerful God, who carries out his purposes—the image the authors obviously wish to establish—it was part of the oral tradition, which the literate redactors were not free to whitewash, however much they might have been tempted.

Of course, for us, with our superior tools of textual analysis, the inconsistencies, the jarringly awkward juxtapositions of one strand of tradition against another, the outright errors all stand out in ways they could have done for no age before our own. But our ability to see how this narrative was constructed over time should not blind us to its immense achievement: mankind's first attempt to write history, a history that mattered deeply because one's whole identity was bound up with it.

For the ancients, the future was always to be a replay of the past, as the past was simply an earthly replay of the drama of the heavens: "History repeats itself"—that is, false history, the history that is not history but myth. For the Jews, history will be no less replete with moral lessons. But the moral is not that history repeats itself but that it is always something new: a process unfolding through time, whose direction and end we cannot know, except insofar as God gives us some hint of what is to come. The future will not be what has happened before; indeed, the only reality that the future has is that it has not happened yet. It is unknowable; and what it will be cannot be discovered by auguries—by reading the stars or examining entrails. We do not control the future; in a profound sense, even God does not control the future because it is the collective responsibility of those who are bringing about the future by their actions in the present. For this reason, the concept of the future—for the first time—holds out promise, rather than just the same old thing. We are not doomed, not bound to some predetermined fate; we are free. If anything can happen, we are truly liberated—as liberated as were the Israelite slaves when they crossed the Sea of Reeds.

This marvelous new sense of time did not descend upon the Israelites all at once. What began as the call of Avraham to leave his place and people and set out for an unknown destiny blossomed into the vocation of Moshe to lead his enslaved people out of the god-haunted ambience of cyclical Egypt, where everything that would be had already been and all important questions had been answered, already set in stone like the staring, immobile statues of Pharaoh. In these two journeys we have gone from the personal (the destiny of Avraham) to the corporate (the destiny of the People of Israel). We have gone from a patronal god, a household god that one carries along for good luck, to YHWH, the God of gods, whose power is mightier even than the mightiest power earth can summon. Taken together, these two great escapes give us an entirely new sense of past and future—the past as constitutive of the present, the future as truly unknown.

But what of the present? Is it just a moment, glinting briefly between past and future, hardly worth elaborating on? No, it is to be the pulsing, white-hot center of all the subsequent narrative, the unlikely intersection of time and eternity, the moment where God is always to be found. This completion of the Jewish religious vision will claim the virtue and intelligence of all the priests, prophets, and kings who will fill the rest of the story of Israel. For it will take all the skill and devotion of this people through all their history to revere the past without adoring it, to bow before the opaque mystery of the future without offering it the fear that is reserved to God alone, and to stand neither in the storied past nor the imagined (or dreaded) future but in the present moment.

This motley band of escaped slaves, revering its memories of distant ancestors who also trudged through the desert, now makes its way from its victorious escape at the seashore to the harsh realities of desert existence. The desert is Sinai, the wedge-shaped peninsula that lies between Egypt and Canaan—and one of our planet's most desolate places. It would be hard to conjure up a landscape more likely to lead to death—a land bereft of all comfort, an earth of so few trees and plants that one may walk for hours without seeing a wisp of green, a place so dry that the uninitiated may die in no time, consumed by what feels like preternatural dehydration. By contrast, the gentler Judean desert of John the Baptist seems almost an oasis.

But this desert brings not death but epiphany, the wildest, most exhausting, most terrifying epiphany of the whole Bible. As the people pass through the wretchedly barren Wilderness of Syn, they grumble repeatedly. They can't find potable water, they are running out of food, now there is no water at all. Each of these complaints God answers to their satisfaction: by making the unpotable water sweet; by giving the people quails and a starch they term *"mahn-hu"*;* by instructing Moshe to strike a rock to bring forth a spring. But despite these miraculous answers to their incessant whining, the people keep regressing, wishing even that they had died in their captivity and longing (in the Bible's memorable phrase) for the fleshpots of Egypt.

Moshe needs God's promptings, because on his own he possesses little political acumen. Even Moshe's father-in-law, Jethro, who shows up at this point, is chagrined by Moshe's sorry lack of organization when he observes him sitting alone, settling every dispute, "while the entire people stations itself around you from daybreak until sunset." Moshe explains that it's up to him to keep the peace, to "judge between a man and his fellow."

But, exclaims Jethro sensibly,

---

* *Mahn-hu,* or "whaddayacallit," which most English Bibles transliterate as "manna" (and is traditionally thought of as "the bread of heaven"), was probably white edible insect secretions to be found on the branches of some rare Sinai plants.

"Not good is this matter, as you do it!
You will become worn out, yes, worn out, so you, this
 people that are with you,
for this matter is too heavy for you,
you cannot do it alone."

As the world's first business consultant, Jethro advises Moshe that he needs a middle-management team so that he can concentrate on priorities:

"So shall it be:
every great matter they shall bring before you,
but every small matter they shall judge by themselves."

Even Jethro's cameo appearance at this point is providential, for the caravans of Israel are now approaching the Mountain, the place where God first spoke to Moshe and promised to do so again. And during the course of this new encounter, during Moshe's absence on the Mountain, we can easily imagine how impossibly chaotic the grumbling people would have become without Moshe's newly appointed middle managers. As we shall see, even with them the people do not show themselves to advantage.

Before Moshe ascends the terrible Mountain, God imparts to him messages of comfort for this fickle people, the reminders they are so constantly in need of:

"You yourselves have seen
what I did in Egypt,

how I bore you on eagles' wings and brought you to me.
So now,
if you will hearken, yes, hearken to my voice
and keep my covenant,
you shall be to me a special-treasure from among all peoples.
Indeed, all the earth is mine,
but you, you shall be to me
a kingdom of priests,
a holy nation."

As will be noted by the early rabbis in their midrash (or commentary), the great God YHWH, who alone has dominion over all, here adopts the posture of a suitor, one who woos a demanding woman, patiently explaining how highly he values her and how exalted he foresees their life together. The people are being prepared for something more than they have already experienced. Moshe knows he must climb the Mountain alone, but God tells him that though he will come to Moshe "in a thick cloud," the people will "hear when I speak to you."

By the time all preparations have been completed—the people purified and instructed not even to touch the Mountain—the trembling Mountain is enveloped in smoke and fire, an active volcano; and it is this sputtering, pulsing apparition that Moshe must approach, the only man worthy to face YHWH. He ascends into the fiery fog. Then, out of nowhere and with no previous hint of what is to come, these words break forth, the great theophany that rings not only down the Mountain to the Chosen People assembled at the

base but down the ages, finding its reverberations in the
hearts of billions of men and women:

"I am YHWH your God,
who brought you out
from the land of Egypt, from a house of serfs.

"You are not to have
any other gods
before my presence.
You are not to make yourself a carved-image
or any figure
that is in the heavens above, that is on the earth beneath,
    that is in the waters beneath the earth;
you are not to bow down to them,
you are not to serve them,
for I, YHWH your God,
am a jealous God,
calling-to-account the iniquity of the fathers upon the sons,
    to the third and fourth (generation)
of those that hate me,
but showing loyalty to the thousandth
of those that love me,
of those that keep my commandments.

"You are not to take up
the name of YHWH your God for emptiness,
for YHWH will not clear him
that takes up his name for emptiness.

"Remember
the Sabbath day, to hallow it.
For six days, you are to serve, and are to make all your
    work,
but the seventh day
is Sabbath for YHWH your God:
you are not to make any kind of work,
(not) you, nor your son, nor your daughter,
(not) your servant, nor your maid, nor your beast,
nor your sojourner that is within your gates.
For six days
YHWH made
the heavens and the earth,
the sea and all that is in it,
and he rested on the seventh day;
therefore YHWH gave the seventh day his blessing, and he
    hallowed it.

"Honor
your father and your mother,
in order that your days may be prolonged
on the soil that YHWH your God is giving you.

"You are not to murder.

"You are not to adulter.

"You are not to steal.

"You are not to testify
against your fellow as a false witness.

"You are not to desire the house of your neighbor;
You are not to desire the wife of your neighbor,
or his servant, or his maid, or his ox, or his donkey,
or anything that is your neighbor's."

Now all the people were seeing
the thunder-sounds,
the flashing-torches,
the *shofar* sound,*
and the mountain smoking;
when the people saw,
they faltered
and stood far off.

The people cry up to Moshe:

"You speak with us, and we will hearken,
but let not God speak with us, lest we die."

And he cries down to them:

"Do not be afraid!
For it is to test you that God has come,
to have awe of him be upon you,
so that you do not sin."

---

* The sound of the ram's horn,
still blown in Jewish ritual.

But the people keep their distance, as Moshe on the heights is swallowed by the storm.

This is the first presentation of the Ten Commandments in the Bible, but because there is a variant—in Deuteronomy 5:6–22—there is no reason to assume that the words quoted here were intended to constitute an exact record of what God said. By submitting these sentences to careful linguistic and textual analysis and comparing them with the variant presentation (which is not *substantially* different), most scholars have come to the conclusion that the original sentences were all bluntly brief in the manner of "You are not to murder"—so brief in fact that each one may have been but one word, that is, a verb in the imperative form preceded by a negative prefix of one syllable. In this way, the originals may actually have been Ten Words—utterly primitive, basic injunctions on the order of "No-kill," "No-steal," "No-lie." These Ten Words (which is the term the Bible uses, not "Commandments") would have been memorizable by even the simplest nomad, his ten fingers a constant reminder of their centrality in his life. So contemporary readers who are repelled by God's vengefulness—his need to punish not only the perpetrator but children, grandchildren, and great-grandchildren—are welcome to take such warnings as the glosses of scribes of a later age.

The exact numbering of the commandments has been a conundrum for aeons. In Jewish medieval tradition, they tended to be broken into five for God (the commandments that mention God's Name) and five for men. Augustine of Hippo in the early fifth century of our era divided them into three for God (by combining the first sentence, God's self-description and not technically a command, with the commandment against idol worship) and seven for men (by breaking the last commandment into two: one for "your neighbor's wife," who appears first in the Deuteronomy list, and a second for "your neighbor's goods"). Augustine's numbering has been followed by the Latin church and by Lutherans and Anglicans. The Greek and other Eastern churches, however, have generally followed what appears to be the most reasonable numbering: four for God (through the Sabbath commandment) and six for men. Since this numbering has been followed by the Reformed churches as well, it is the numbering one is most likely to encounter in the United States.

But this attention to minutiae (which of the words are original? how should we divide the text to achieve ten?) can, like so many scholarly considerations, deflect us all too easily from appreciating what is happening here. There is no document in all the literatures of the world that is like the Ten Commandments. Of course, there are ethical guidelines from other cultures. But these are always offered in a legal framework (if you do that, then this will be the consequence) or as worldly-wise advice (if you want to lead a happy life, you will be sure to do such-and-such and avoid so-and-so). Here for the first—and, I think, the last—time, human beings are offered a code without justification. Because this is God's code, no justification is required and (except for the few poor phrases of scribal commentary) no elaboration. Who but God can speak ten words—"Thou-shalt" and "Thou-shalt-not"—with such authority that no further words are needed?

There is an almost perfect story by G. K. Chesterton about a jewel thief who is pursued by a priest—a very confident jewel thief, Flambeau, and a very humble parish priest, Father Brown, who understands human hearts because he knows the sinfulness of his own. Toward the story's end, the priest finds himself on Hampstead Heath, looking up admiringly at the heavens as night descends and sitting next to the jewel thief, who is blissfully unaware that this bumbling little parson is his pursuer. Flambeau, who is also dressed as a priest in order to steal a precious object of religious art—the "Blue Cross" that gives the story its name—scorns with what he imagines to be priestly piety the attitudes of "modern infidels," who "appeal to their reason." Looking up at the sky, now spangled with stars, he continues: "But who can look at those millions of worlds and not feel that there may well be wonderful universes above us where reason is utterly unreasonable?"

"Reason and justice," replies Father Brown, "grip the remotest and the loneliest star. Look at those stars. Don't they look as if they were single diamonds and sapphires? Well, you can imagine any mad botany or geology you please. Think of forests of adamant with leaves of brilliants. Think, the moon is a blue moon, a single elephantine sapphire. But don't fancy that all that frantic astronomy would make the smallest difference to the reason and justice of conduct. On plains of opal, under cliffs cut out of pearl, you would still find a notice-board, 'Thou shalt not steal.' "

Father Brown is alluding, of course, to the famous absoluteness of the Ten Commandments. They require no justification, nor can they be argued away. They are not dependent upon circumstances, nor may they be set aside because of special considerations. They are not propositions for debate. They are not suggestions. They are not even (as a recent book would have us imagine in the jargon of our day) "ten challenges." They are exactly what they seem to be—and there is no getting around them or (to be more spatially precise) out from under them. But the only thing new about them is their articulation at this moment amid the terrifying fires of Sinai. They have been received by billions as reasonable, necessary, even unalterable because they are written on human hearts and always have been. They were always there in the inner core of the human person—in the deep silence that each of us carries within. They needed only to be spoken aloud.

The age to which these Ten Words were first spoken was a brutal one, an age of spiteful goddesses and cruel god-kings (not a bit like our own). The people who first heard these words were unrefined and basic, the Dusty Ones, wandering through Sinai's lunar landscape, denuded of the ordinary web of life, baked in absolute heat and merciless light. This was no age or people or environment for anything but the plainest, harshest truths. We should not be surprised that these words were never spoken to the powerful, the comfortable, and the subtle. This was the time, this the place, these the people who must receive the unassailable truth of the Ten Words and carry them forward.

Readers who do not believe in God may well have reached the end of their rope by now. For surely the first commandments—the ones about God—will strike them not as unassailable but as meaningless. But let the unbeliever focus on the commandments about man and ask himself which he would drop and what he would add. Here, I think, both believer and unbeliever are brought to heel. There is nothing to add, really, nothing to subtract. Oh, I could add something about ecology perhaps or about racism or sexism or, if I were of such a mind, about the sacredness of free markets or the solidarity of the human race—all concerns born of recent times. But if I can peer through the mists of history and see the begrimed, straightforward faces straining upward toward the terrors of Mount Sinai and if I can imagine this immense throng of simple souls trudging through the whole of history—all the ordinary people down the ages in need of moral guidance in all the incredibly various situations and cultures that this planet has known—it must be admitted that it would be fairly impossible to improve on the Decalogue as we have it. The sins it catalogues are the great sins, and those it does not mention explicitly—such as withholding sustenance from those who have nothing—can be deduced from it, which is what the Israelites did almost immediately by, for instance, categorizing society's abandonment of widows and orphans as "murder." Even as far away from Sinai in time and civilization as Hampstead Heath at the turn of the century or Central Park at the turn of the millennium, there are few who do not know that if we were to keep these commandments our world would be an entirely different place. This is such a simple, incontestable thing to *say* that it sounds banal. But for all our resourcefulness we have never yet managed to *do* it.

Besides the innovation of speaking the unspoken moral law aloud, one should note the lesser—but hardly unimportant—innovation of the weekend, which got its start in the Jewish Sabbath (or "Ceasing"). No ancient society before the Jews had a day of rest. The God who made the universe and rested bids us do the same, calling us to a weekly restoration of prayer, study, and recreation (or re-creation). In this study (or *talmud*), we have the beginnings of what Nahum Sarna has called "the universal duty of continuous self-education," Israel being the first human society to so value education and the first to envision it as a universal pursuit—and a democratic obligation that those in power must safeguard on behalf of those in their employ. The connections to both freedom and creativity lie just beneath the surface of this commandment: leisure is appropriate to a free people, and this people so recently free find themselves quickly establishing this quiet weekly celebration of their freedom; leisure is the necessary ground of creativity, and a free people are free to imitate the creativity of God. The Sabbath is surely one of the simplest and sanest recommendations any god has ever made; and those who live without such septimanal punctuation are emptier and less resourceful.

The patriarchs are present here at Sinai, for we now have

in these commandments a codification of the Abrahamic covenant of blood. Circumcision was the outward sign of this covenant; the Commandments are the invisible sign, circumcision of the heart. God will be their God, and they will be his people, his kingdom of priests, his holy nation, if only they will keep his Commandments. This is an exclusive relationship, which specifically excludes bedding down with strange gods. As the medieval rabbis noted, it is very like a marriage. As modern commentators have noted, it is very like a typical suzerainty treaty between contracting parties in the ancient Near East—like the pact Avraham made with the Canaanite kings—but the big difference is that in this case the king is God.

Of the many innovations that Sinai represents—the codification of Abrahamic henotheism (that one God is to be worshiped, even though others are presumed to exist), the articulation of "ought-ness" (or what Kant will one day call the "categorical imperative"), the invention of the Sabbath—nothing is as provocative as the way in which this tremendous theophany brings to completion the new Israelite understanding of time. The journey of Avraham and the liberation wrought by Moshe transformed human understanding of past and future: the past is all the steps of my forebears and myself that have brought me to this place and moment; the future is what is yet to be. But the past is irretrievable and the future is a blank. The one is fixed, the other unknown. For the past I can have only regret, for the future only anxiety. To live in real time, to live in history, can be a horrible experience—and no wonder that the ancients contrived to escape such torments by inventing cyclical time and the recurrent Wheel, leading only to the peace of death.

But this gift of the Commandments allows us to live in the present, in the here and now. What I have done in the past is past mending; what I will do in the future is a worry not worth the candle, for there is no way I can know what will happen next. But in this moment—and only in this moment—I am in control. This is the moment of choice, the moment when I decide whether I will plunge in the knife or not, take the treasure or not, begin to spin the liar's web or not. This is the moment when the past can be transformed and the future lit with radiance. And such a realization need bring neither regret nor anxiety but, if I keep the Commandments, true peace. But not the peace of death, not the peace of coming to terms with the Wheel. For in choosing what is right I am never more alive.

The standard of the Ten Words gradually gives to subsequent Israelite history a reliability and consistency of texture that we search for in vain in other ancient cultures. In all the ancient epics left to us, the dwelling places of the gods—the heavenly realms of ultimate reality—prove to be shifting and insubstantial. Zeus is driven by his insatiable lusts, Ishtar by her fathomless ill humor; and we earthlings are at the mercy of their incomprehensible heavenly mood swings. Even these hapless earthbound wanderers, the Israelites, were people of the ancient world; and they tended to give their God YHWH a human personality—a jealousy that makes him seem at times not unlike the difficult gods of alien pantheons. But the gulf that has opened between the worldview of Israel and that of all other ancient societies will only widen as time goes on.

It is important at this juncture to take full account not only of the primitive quality of the Ten—their almost caveman awkwardness—but also of their wonderful flexibility. This is because, like any effective declaration or constitution, they do not say too much, which enables them to be elaborated and interpreted by later ages in contexts that would have been unimaginable at the foot of Mount Sinai. We have already noted Israel's interpretation of the murder prohibition as including an obligation in justice to have-nots. Throughout history no commandment will receive more attention or be more hotly debated than this one, used even in our own day by left-wingers and right-wingers, by pacifists and pro-lifers, by anti-death-penalty activists and death-penalty advocates, as their ultimate justification. But whether you are president of the Joint Chiefs or of the Fellowship of Reconciliation, a supporter of Right to Life or of NARAL, Jesse Helms or Helen Prejean, you would hardly urge the scrapping or suppression of this commandment.

Another aspect of this bare-knuckled theophany that should give pause to those who believe in an afterlife is its paucity of rewards. Long life is promised to those who take care of their parents, but *eternal* life is promised to no one. No one had even thought of such a thing, except as a fanciful and impossible goal, as in the *Epic of Gilgamesh,* for

> When the gods created mankind
> They appointed death for mankind,
> Kept eternal life in their own hands.

Even the promise of long life is almost certainly a later accretion. As had never been the case before—and as would never be so starkly the case again—virtue is its own reward. I must obey these commands because they must be obeyed.

Something in human beings resists all this, leaving one wanting to respond truculently, "Oh, yeah? That's what *you* think, YHWH!" "It is religion itself which we all by nature dislike, not the excess merely," said John Henry Newman. "Nature tends toward the earth, and God is in heaven." And surely nothing is less appealing than a religion of unappealable commands. Nothing so quickly provokes the urge to sin as an extended meditation on virtue. And, this being so, we can hardly raise an eyebrow at what happens next.

The Children of Israel waste no time in breaking as many Commandments as possible. Exasperated by Moshe's long absence on the Mountain, they regress. They pressure Aharon to *do* something—and his knee-jerk solution is to return to the easy comforts of the ancient worldview: he collects the gold jewelry that the Israelites absconded with, melts it down, and fashions an idol, a visible sign for the anxious people to worship. Exodus calls it "a molten calf," though this is by way of denigrating the idol. It was actually a bull, probably rampant and in rut, the aboriginal symbol of potency. This, cries Aharon,

"This is your God, O Israel,
who brought you up from the land of Egypt!"

What follows is an orgy of prostrations, animal slaughter, feasting, drinking, and, as the Book of Exodus puts it discreetly, "reveling"—that is, sexual indulgence in the manner of a pagan liturgy. The bull, as we have seen, was a common image of divinity in Mesopotamia, as it was in Egypt; and though we cannot be certain that the people thought they were worshiping a bull-god (they may only have meant to worship YHWH as the invisible God who stands on the bull as his footstool), they have surely made "a carved image" of a visible figure. They have mistaken YHWH for his creation. They have broken the first two Commandments. They have also dishonored their forebears—their ancient fathers and mothers—who had so long refrained from idol worship; and, in the course of their reveling, it is most unlikely that they managed to refrain from adultery and sexual covetousness. With a little ingenuity, we might even conclude that they succeeded in breaking all Ten Commandments—but even five out of ten is a pretty good average for so short a time.

Meanwhile, back on Mount Sinai, Moshe, who now has the Ten Words in written form—"the two tablets of Testimony"*—is told by God that

---

* It is the mention of *two* tablets that encouraged later commentators to assume a division of the Commandments into two kinds, those concerning God and those concerning man. But the two tablets probably hark back to the treaty conventions of the ancient Middle East, with one copy intended for each party to the agreement, just as we provide in contracts to this day. What writing system the Ten could have been written in and who could have read them are unanswerable questions. The alphabet is a Semitic invention, developed in the Levant by Phoenician scribes. Its stupendous advantage over the earlier Sumerian and Egyptian systems, which required mastery of thousands of symbols, lies in its simplicity, which allows it to be learned by anyone, not just the cultivated and leisurely. It represents, therefore, a giant step toward democratization (and it would over the ensuing centuries be copied with variations by Greeks and Romans). But whether Moshe, who would have known hieroglyphics (from which the Semitic scribes borrowed most of the forms for their new system), could have been aware of such a system (which did, indeed, exist by the likely date of Exodus), we just don't know.

"your people
whom you brought up from the
   land of Egypt
has wrought ruin!"

The Covenant has already been broken—as it were, minutes after it was made. The people are no longer God's but Moshe's. God calls them "stiff-necked" (in King James; "hard-necked" in Fox, like the hard-hearted Pharaoh), and he asks Moshe's leave to destroy them. He will use Moshe alone to "make into a great nation," as he used Noah after the Flood.

For the first time (but hardly for the last) God's chosen representative argues with him:

"For-what-reason,
O YHWH,
should your anger flare out against
   your people

whom you brought out of the land of Egypt
with great power,
with a strong hand?
For-what-reason should the Egyptians (be able to) say, yes,
   say:
'With evil intent he brought them out,
to kill them in the mountains,
to destroy them from the face of the soil'?
Turn away from your flaming anger,
be sorry for the evil (intended) against your people!
Recall Avraham, Yitzhak and Yisrael your servants,
to whom you swore by yourself
when you spoke to them:
'I will make your seed many
as the stars of the heavens,
and all this land which I have promised,
I will give to your seed,
that they may inherit (it) for the ages!' "
And YHWH let himself be sorry concerning the evil
that he had spoken of doing to his people.

Well, the truth is that YHWH *is* something of a bull—and
he shouldn't be so surprised that the people have decided to
picture him thus. It is obvious that at this period—a period
in which this odd little phyla of Semites is ever so gradually
evolving from polytheists to monotheists—they are attributing to their favorite God the qualities of other principal
Middle Eastern deities: he is a storm god, who appears in
heavenly fire and fog and whose angers, like his thunder-

bolts, are sudden and destructive, fulminating and volcanic (like Vulcan, fire god of the Romans). As we shall see, these depictions of divine wrath will eventually give way to a purer understanding of God, but at this moment we have a snapshot of monotheism in its tadpole stage.

It should also be noted that God's portrayal of the Israelites as "stiff-necked" will one day serve as the dominant note in Christian caricatures of Jews. It will be Shylock's "stiff-necked" and literalist adherence to an outmoded morality of revenge that will enable Shakespeare to cast him in so unfavorable a light. The assumption will be that Jews, because of their moral vision of an unforgiving God, do not forgive but always insist on their "pound of flesh." It is this supposedly "Jewish" quality that will serve as a fundamental justification for the anti-Jewish attitudes that so infected the Middle Ages—right up to the late modern period, when new theories of racial inferiority made it possible for medieval anti-Hebraism (which was basically a kind of character assassination) to be replaced by the more horrifyingly effective weapon of "scientific" anti-Semitism.

What is ghoulishly fascinating about the history of Christian depictions of Jews (even as early as the fourth century A.D. in the elegantly vicious sermons of John Chrysostom) is that the people being excoriated are presumed to exhibit the unyielding qualities of God himself—the same God whom Christians claimed to worship and whose sacred scriptures they revered. A good case can be made that medieval anti-Hebraism and its modern offspring anti-Semitism are both forms of God-hatred, masquerading as self-justifying intolerance. The hatred of Christians for Jews may have its ultimate source in hatred of God, a hatred that the hater must carefully keep himself from knowing about. Why would one hate God? To find the answer we probably need look no further than the stark, unyielding Ten.

Following hard on the revelation of the Ten come interminable series of prescriptions which fill most of the rest of the Torah* and are understood to this day by observant Jews as the heart of the Torah. They did not issue from Sinai, though the final compilers (in the fifth century B.C., six centuries after the desert theophany) would have us believe so. They have been shoehorned in, gracelessly interrupting the narrative with insertions meant to govern the activities of a people long settled on their land, not the wanderers of Sinai. And their language is the language of lawyers and priests, not storytellers. One prescription, called *lex talionis,* the law of retaliation ("eye for eye, tooth for tooth, hand for hand, foot for foot"), has often been used to demonstrate the harshness of "Old" Testament morality and

* The Torah (or "Teaching," sometimes translated inadequately as "Law") is the name Jews give to the first five books of the Bible. (For more information, see "The Books of the Hebrew Bible" at the end of this book.) The Torah is like a great mosaic, and though its simple underlying pattern may be attributed to one artist (according to later tradition, Moshe himself) its intricate parts and complex impression are the work of many hands. Despite what I take to be the essential historicity of this material, it is hardly without special agendas. Patched into the narrative of the Egyptian captivity, for instance, are ritual prescriptions that date to a much later time, when Israel was long settled in Canaan and its priests had the leisure to develop intricate rubrics. In this way, the Passover Lamb and the prescriptions concerning the matzahs (or unleavened bread to be used at the Passover Seder), which stemmed originally from springtime agricultural festivals, were added at a much later date to the original narrative, because the priests wanted the great story of liberation as justification for their rituals.

its commonality with the laws of Sumer—and, in fact, the *lex talionis* appears in the Code of Hammurabi, many centuries before its repetition here.

It is true that one finds in the Torah many laws that can only make us wince: "Thou shalt not suffer a witch to live" has been used repeatedly in Western history to get rid of inconvenient old women, as at Salem, Massachusetts; and the commands in Leviticus to execute homosexuals and burn alive both the perpetrator of incest and his victims are unlikely to commend themselves to modern ears. But it is also true that this long-winded, unwieldy compilation of assorted prescriptions represents an overall softening—a humanizing—of the common law of the ancient Middle East, which easily prescribed a hand not for a hand but for the theft of a loaf of bread or for the striking of one's better and which gave much favor to the rights of the nobility and virtually none to the lower classes. The casual cruelty of other ancient law codes—the cutting off of nose, ears, tongue, lower lip (for kissing another man's wife), breasts, and testicles—is seldom matched in the Torah. Rather, in the prescriptions of Jewish law we cannot but note a presumption that all people, even slaves, are human and that all human lives are sacred. The constant bias is in favor not of the powerful and their possessions but of the powerless and their poverty; and there is even a frequent enjoinder to sympathy:

> "A sojourner you are not to oppress:
> you yourselves know (well) the feelings of the sojourner,
> for sojourners were you in the land of Egypt."

This bias toward the underdog is unique not only in ancient law but in the whole history of law. However faint our sense of justice may be, insofar as it operates at all it is still a Jewish sense of justice.

The link between the mainstream traditions of the Western world and the traditions of the Jews shows itself at its weakest when we consider the many prescriptions in the Torah that will come to serve as the basis for *halakha,* the body of Jewish prescriptive law that is meant to govern every aspect of life and that has grown to enormous proportions from the late classical period to the present. A single sentence in Exodus, for instance—"You are not to boil a kid in the milk of its mother," probably a proscription against cruelty—will become the basis for a large portion of Jewish dietary laws about keeping all meat and fowl separate from all milk and milk-based foods, even to the complication of maintaining two sets of dishes and kitchen implements. Such laws, elaborated from the prescriptions of the Torah, then expanded in the Mishna, the early rabbinic law code of the late second century of our era, then interpreted further in the Talmuds of the early medieval period and reinterpreted further in (often obscurantist) rabbinic commentaries down to our day, have never gained much influence beyond the relatively small circles of observant Jews, never entered the mainstream of Western consciousness and ideas—so they are largely beyond the purview of this book. The endless legal refinements made down the centuries by the rabbis have given the word *talmudic* the connotation of "differentiating to the point of absurdity." They have also set Jew against

Jew, so that we hear even in our day the invidious charge of the super-Orthodox that more flexible forms of Judaism aren't Judaism.

But, even at their most hairsplittingly bizarre, these laws remain testimony to the fact that the Jews were the first people to develop an integrated view of life and its obligations. Rather than imagining the demands of law and the demands of wisdom as discrete realms (as did the Sumerians, the Egyptians, and the Greeks), they imagined that all of life, having come from the Author of life, was to be governed by a single outlook. The material and the spiritual, the intellectual and the moral were one:

> Hearken O Israel:
> YHWH our God, YHWH (is) One!

The great formula is not that there is one God but that "God is One." From this insight will flow not only the integrating and universalist propensities of Western philosophy but even the possibility of modern science. For life is not a series of discrete experiences, influenced by diverse forces. We do not live in a fragmented universe, controlled by fickle and warring gods. As Bob Dylan sings:

> Ring them bells, sweet Martha,
> for the poor man's son.
> Ring them bells so the world will know
> that God is one.

God and "the poor man's son" belong together. Because God is One, life is a moral continuum—and reality makes sense.

Bloodshed follows the orgy of betrayal. Moshe descends from the Mountain, the two tablets of the Ten Words in his hands, hears "the sound of choral-song"—the antiphonal chanting characteristic of ancient liturgy—and sees "the calf and the dancing," at which

> Moshe's anger flared up,
> he threw the tablets from his hands
> and smashed them beneath the mountain.

The Covenant is now literally broken. Moshe melts down the idol and grinds it to powder, which he mixes with water, and forces the Children of Israel to drink the vile mixture. Then, rounding on Aharon, he almost beseeches him to exonerate himself, which Aharon manages dextrously:

> "Let not my lord's anger flare up!
> You yourself know this people, how set-on-evil it is.
> They said to me: 'Make us a god who will go before us,
> for Moshe, the man who brought us up from the land of
> Egypt,
> we do not know what has become of him!'
> So I said to them: 'Who has gold?'
> They broke it off and gave it to me,

I threw it into the fire, and out came this calf."
Now when Moshe saw the people: that it had gotten–loose,
for Aharon had let-it-loose for whispering among their foes,
Moshe took-up-a-stand at the gate of the camp
and said:
"Whoever is for YHWH—to me!
Thus says YHWH, the God of Israel:
'Put every-man his sword on his thigh,
proceed and go back–and-forth from gate to gate in the
     camp,
and kill
every-man his brother, every-man his neighbor, every-man
     his relative!' "
The Sons of Levi did according to Moshe's words.
And there fell of the people on that day some three
     thousand men.

Is there a way to understand this passage about a God who
has hardly finished issuing an absolute command against
murder when he delivers the command for a general slaughter? Moshe was leader of a primitive desert tribe, set on open
rebellion. There were no courts to appeal to, no law besides
the word of YHWH and Moshe's resolve to enforce it. Had
he not allied himself with the sword-wielding sons of Levi,
the Exodus story might have ended right here. There are
also in this episode hints of later factionalism—of the northern Levitical priests in competition with the Aharonid
priesthood, which would come to control the Jerusalem
Temple in the south—a rivalry that is retrojected into this

narrative. But the slaughter oppresses the reader's spirit. We can tell ourselves as often as we like that this was a primitive people who needed to be dealt with harshly or that the episode can be explained by later social tensions. We still need to understand why God is enshrined in this narrative as demanding slaughter. There may be no answer, except the answer of Augustine of Hippo: "We are talking about God. Which wonder do you think you understand? If you understand, it is not God."

But there are many mysteries in the text of Exodus that do not demand a resort to mystagogy—mysteries that are basically textual. Moshe's ascents and descents are hard to keep track of; and it is his disappearance into the smoke on the Mountain's summit for forty days that makes the Israelites desperate and provokes their backsliding. Puzzling (even sometimes exasperating) to a modern reader are the interruptions of the narrative by lengthy later insertions—elaborations of the original Ten; rules for farmers and herders; detailed rubrics for building an ark (or portable cabinet) that will enclose the tablets (Moshe eventually ends up with a second set) and for the "tent of meeting" that will serve as shelter for the ark when Israel is encamped.

Despite the thinning of their numbers, the Children of Israel do not improve. They lose heart at the least reversal, their complaints are never-ending, their quickness to revolt a constant threat to the whole enterprise. After putting up with their yammering for a couple of years, God decides to make them wander the Sinai for a full forty years before settlement in Canaan, in this way ensuring that the whole generation of Egyptian-bred complainers will die out and be replaced by a more rugged generation, hardened by wilderness trials—born nomads who expect always to journey on, rather than displaced city mice longing for the remembered fleshpots.

One of the most remarkable features of the Torah narrative—and a feature evidenced in no other ancient literature—is a hypersensitivity to the decisive influence of environment and its ability to shape both conscience and consciousness. Neither Sumer nor Egypt is ever described; from the Bible alone we would know virtually nothing of the first, and of the second mainly that its king was a fool who thought he could withstand the Real God. Any good museum of art can give us a better sense of these ancient societies than does the Bible, which actually sprang from these lush cultural sources. We can walk through an exhibition, admiring the golden statues of the pharaohs and the winged gods of Babylon without the least inclination to incline the head or bow the knee. But the Bible is a believer's history, not a history of art or culture, and one that was all too close to the temptations of Egypt's fleshpots and Sumer's hieratic cruelties. Its authors felt no need to indulge in literary descriptions of civilized luxury, for cult and culture were so wedded in the ancient world that any appreciation of the cultural values of Egypt or Sumer (and, later, Babylon) could only tempt weak and wayward Israelites from the difficult way of the living God to the easy worship of the Golden Calf.

It is no accident, therefore, that the great revelations of God's own Name and of his Commandments occur in a mountainous desert, as far from civilization and its contents as possible, in a place as unlike the lush predictabilities and comforts of the Nile and the Euphrates as this earth of ours can offer. If God—the Real God, the One God—was to speak to human beings and if there was any possibility of their hearing him, it could happen only in a place stripped of all cultural reference points, where even nature (which was so imbued with contrary, god-inhabited forces) seemed absent. Only amid inhuman rock and dust could this fallible collection of human beings imagine becoming human in a new way. Only under a sun without pity, on a mountain devoid of life, could the living God break through the cultural filters that normally protect us from him. "YHWH, YHWH," he thunders at Moshe, the man alone on the Mountain:

> "God,
> showing-mercy, showing-favor,
> long-suffering in anger,
> abundant in loyalty and faithfulness,
> keeping loyalty to the thousandth (generation),
> bearing iniquity, rebellion and sin,
> yet not clearing, clearing (the guilty),
> calling-to-account the iniquity of the fathers upon the sons
>   and upon sons' sons, to the third and fourth
>   (generation)!"

This is God's self-description, the one he would have us remember. He is the God of mercy and forgiveness, the God who never deserts his people, faithful to the end, patient with all our failings however dismaying, but reminding us that a household—a familial environment, holding three (or sometimes four) generations—cannot escape the sins of the oldest generation; they necessarily infect the atmosphere.

Moshe, the medium for this revelation, is both God's representative and the people's. To God he speaks on the people's behalf, to the people on God's behalf. His is a far more difficult calling than that of Avraham, who was almost a Sumerian Odysseus—a man with a mission, all right, but a wily character who seemed up to any challenge. Moshe is a man who does not think highly of himself, who never relies on his own talents, only on God's word. He was, as Exodus says of him, "the humblest man on earth," an extraordinary description in a world of boastful heroes. In his humility he has been hollowed out like a reed, so that there is nothing in him—no pride or quirk of personality—to distort God's message. He can serve, therefore, as an authentic medium, a true channel.

The difference between the two great figures of Judaism's beginnings constitutes additional evidence of their essential historical authenticity. Both men are alike in that they were settled and prosperous but called to be nomads—to wander over many years without any timetable for eventual settlement. But if their stories were simply the myths of an oral Semitic culture, we would find it hard to distinguish between them, for they serve such similar functions. We cannot know how many Sumerian businessmen God may have tried to speak to before Avram heard his voice. Nor can we know how many Hebrews, engaged in building Egyptian cities like Rameses, may have heard a troubling voice before they flicked it away like a fly and returned to their bricks. But Moshe, building on the cherished ancestral stories of a God who spoke to men, is able to add new definition and concreteness of detail to this revelation—of a God who leads his pilgrim people, refusing to desert them despite their appalling limitations.

The family god of Avraham, the Terror of Yitzhak, the Angel who wrestled all night with Israel, has become the God of a *people,* the Israelites, whom he means to guard like a jealous husband. But he is more than the God of Israel, for he is the universal God, the Creator of all, who has deigned in his mysterious mercy to single out this people and make them his holy nation. Everything proceeds from the double revelation of Sinai, the covenant of the Ten Words and the revelation of God's essential self: He-Who-Is, He-Who-Will-Be-There.

The fire of Sinai, both in the revelation of the Ten and in the revelation of the Name, will not desert Israel, but will gradually be reconfigured from a symbol of the storm god's anger to the refining fire of God's love:

We only live, only suspire
Consumed by either fire or fire,

wrote T. S. Eliot. We must be consumed either by the anger of the storm god or by the love of the living God. There is no way around life and its sufferings. Our only choice is whether we will be consumed by the fire of our own heedless fears and passions or allow God to refine us in his fire and to shape us into a fitting instrument for his revelation, as he did Moshe. We need not fear God as we fear all other suffering, which burns and maims and kills. For God's fire, though it will perfect us, will not destroy, for "the bush was not consumed."

This insight into God is the unearthly illumination that will light up all the greatest works of subsequent Western literature. From the psalms of David and the prophecies of Isaiah to the visions of Dante and the dreams of Dostoevsky, the bush will burn but will not be consumed. As Allen Ginsberg will one day write, "The only poetic tradition is the voice out of the burning bush."

FIVE

CANAAN

✴

From Tribe to Nation

Deuteronomy, the fifth and last book of the Torah, ends on an elegiac note, full of the sadness that all true endings possess. Moshe is standing on the peak of Mount Nebo in Transjordan, looking out across the Dead Sea and the River Jordan to Canaan, the Promised Land that he will never enter. He can see the whole land of the Promise, from Dan in the north to the Mediterranean Sea in the west to the Negev desert in the south. Opposite him across the river is Jericho, Moon City, "the city of palms" according to Deuteronomy—the oldest town on earth.

And YHWH said to him:
"This is the land
that I swore to Avraham, to Yitzhak, and to Yaakov, saying:
'To your seed I give it!'
I have let you see it with your eyes,
but there you shall not cross!"

So there died there Moshe, servant of YHWH,
in the land of Moav,
at the order of YHWH.
He buried him
in a valley in the land of Moav,
opposite Bet Pe'or,
and no man has knowledge of the site of his burial-place
    until this day.

Now Moshe was a hundred and twenty years old at his
    death;
his eyes had not grown-dim,
his vigor had not fled.
The Children of Israel wept for Moshe in the Plains of
    Moav for thirty days.
Then the days of weeping in mourning for Moshe were
    ended.

Now Yehoshua [Joshua] son of Nun was filled with the
    spirit of wisdom,
for Moshe had leaned his hands upon him,*
and (so) the Children of Israel hearkened to him
and did as YHWH had commanded Moshe.
But there arose no further prophet in Israel like Moshe,
whom YHWH knew face to face,
in all the signs and portents
that YHWH sent him to do in the land of Egypt,
to Pharaoh and to all his servants, and to all his land;
and in all the strong hand
and in all the great, awe-inspiring (acts)
that Moshe did before the eyes of all Israel.

---

* To lean (or lay) hands on
someone by embracing his head was
thought to make vital power pass
from one person to another. In the
case of a great leader, this enabled
the charism of leadership to pass
from the leader to his successor.

To a large extent, the lives of
Moshe and his patriarchal predecessors must remain opaque to
us, almost as opaque as the lives
of our dimmest ancestors, the

hominids of prehistory. We know they looked up at the night sky in wonder, wandered ceaselessly with only a vague notion of a destination, and heard the promptings of an inner voice, which they associated with the terrifying marvels of nature. But the harsh and singular specifics of their lives were quite unlike our own, we who can scarcely close our ears to the ceaseless din of modern advertising, who never venture far from the familiar, for whom the night sky, eclipsed by round-the-clock electricity, is no longer a marvel at all.

But in this ending, in the death of Moshe, we can feel a basic human kinship beneath the dramatic differences. The description of the still vigorous old man must recall to us the ancient grandeur of Michelangelo's Moses, huge-armed, straight-backed, eagle-eyed, who after so many harrowing meetings with God and disappointments with his people can face death without flinching. We, too, shall die without finishing what we began. Each of us has in our life at least one moment of insight, one Mount Sinai—an uncanny, otherworldly, time-stopping experience that somehow succeeds in breaking through the grimy, boisterous present, the insight that, if we let it, will carry us through our life. But like Moshe or Martin Luther King, though we may remember that we "have been to the mountaintop," we do not enter the Promised Land, but only glimpse it fleetingly. "Nothing that is worth doing," wrote Reinhold Niebuhr, "can be achieved in our lifetime, therefore we must be saved by hope. Nothing which is true or beautiful or good makes complete sense in any immediate context of history; therefore we must be saved by faith. Nothing we do, however virtuous, can be accomplished alone; therefore we must be saved by love." That accomplishment is intergenerational may be the deepest of all Hebrew insights.

I t is Joshua, Moshe's young general, who leads the Israelites across the Jordan into the Promised Land with the ark at their head, Joshua first sending his men through the camp with these instructions: "When you see the ark of the covenant of YHWH your God being carried by the levitical priests, you will leave your position and follow it, so that you may know which way to take, since you have never gone this way before." This is the great moment, the moment of maximum anticipation—to go the way one has never gone before, and yet to go home:

> The ole ark's a-moverin', moverin', moverin',
> The ole ark's a-moverin',
> An' I'm goin' home!

And as we know from another rousing African American spiritual, it is not long before Jericho is defeated, its walls collapsing at the sound of Joshua's trumpets:

> Joshua fit de battle ob Jericho, Jericho, Jericho,
> Joshua fit de battle ob Jericho,
> And de walls come tumblin' down.

Perhaps no one in all history has understood the liberation narrative of Israel as profoundly—and with such affection and joy—as the black slaves of the American South. There is even evidence that something like the destruction of Jericho may have occurred, since archaeologists have found that several Palestinian towns were flattened about the year 1200 B.C., to be succeeded by a new culture that from a material point of view was decidedly inferior—and may represent the Israelite occupation of ruined Canaanite settlements. But Jericho's ruin apparently preceded Israel's invasion of Canaan by centuries; and it may be that its ruined walls encouraged the Israelites of a later period to imagine that they had been its conquerors.

The conquest of Canaan, as presented in the Book of Joshua (which brings the Epic of Israel—from founding patriarch to final settlement—to its conclusion) is a grisly business, reminding us of just how primitive a society we have been considering. All the Canaanites—"men and women, young and old, oxen, sheep, and donkeys"—are put to the sword, their settlements burned to the ground, their objects of precious metal set aside as "holy," "devoted" to the sanctuary of YHWH—that is, priestly booty. The Canaanites, too, are set aside as "devoted"—that is, marked for extermination. As far away from the Jordan valley as prehistoric Scotland, the sacrificial victim, the prisoner of war offered to a god, was called the "Devoted One." What we have here is human sacrifice under the guise of holy war, compelling us to recognize how powerful a hold the need to scapegoat and to shed blood has on the human heart.

But this legendary "conquest," described with such bloodthirsty relish in Joshua as an overwhelming victory, was actually a very gradual affair. From its base in Transjordan, the tribes that Moshe had led through the desert migrated into the central hill country of Canaan, overwhelming its Iron Age settlements when possible, but at other times entering into league with Canaanite villagers, sometimes to overthrow an oppressive tyrant, at other times in mutual protection pacts. Egypt's Dusty Ones and Moshe's kvetchers had indeed been toughened by adversity and now presented themselves as impressive warriors whom peaceful farmers had better not tangle with. Cutting a swath of conquest across a small area, these warriors no doubt attracted many new adherents to the religion of their conquering God, adherents who came to see themselves as Israelites, the people of YHWH, the God who could humble even Egypt.

But cultural exchange is seldom a one-way affair. After settling the central highlands and intermingling with the natives, "the Israelites then did what is evil in YHWH's eyes and served the Baals." Baal was the Canaanite storm god, who must have seemed rather like YHWH to unlettered Israelites, so what the hell. "To serve the Baals" was to worship one of Baal's many images, metal bulls and phallic stones erected at various sanctuaries throughout Canaan. Baal's consort was Astarte, the Canaanite form of the Mesopotamian fertility goddess Ishtar. Astarte (or Astoreth) was also called Asherah, a word that probably means "consort." The pure religion of YHWH, under the influence of these local superstitions of vegetative, animal, and human fertility, was often to be compromised and combined with Canaanite cults in unexpected ways. Inscriptions have been discovered dating to the period of the monarchy, a couple of centuries after Joshua, that seem to be prayers to "YHWH and his Asherah," leading many to the conclusion that the desert religion of YHWH underwent a kind of paganizing syncretism as soon as the hardened Hebrew warriors settled down to the business of farming and herding among their Canaanite neighbors.

The period after Joshua's invasion is called the period of the Judges—local military leaders who also settled disputes between Israelites in the manner of Moshe's desert judges. As described in the Book of Judges, this appears to have been a time of continuing settlement and consolidation, in which Israelite warrior-farmers gradually spread out through Canaan in loose tribal confederations till in less than two centuries they occupied most of the Promised Land. In the Books of Joshua and Judges, success is invariably linked to Israel's faithfulness to YHWH, defeat to their prostituting themselves to "other gods . . . of the surrounding peoples."

Despite the overall success of the settlement, the Israelites are never without enemies, especially the growing menace of the Philistines, the Sea People, who after the collapse of Mycene sailed across the Mediterranean and began to occupy coastal towns such as Gaza, then inland towns such as Gath. Their encroachments brought them uncomfortably close to the Israelites, who sometimes found themselves living in Philistine towns under the boot of these enemies, whose name will come to mean "crude and uncultivated" and will serve as the basis for the word "Palestine." (The story of Samson, the magnificent Israelite strongman who harried the Philistines, belongs to this period.) At last, the Israelites reach the conclusion that what they need is someone to give them visible unity, someone capable of uniting them in greater emotional cohesion—a king.

But YHWH is their king. Since the days of the *qahal,* the desert assembly of the pilgrim people, Israel's political understanding has been that they are the gathering of God's people, led by his handpicked spokesmen and answerable to no earthly king, a sort of theocratic democracy. "Obey the voice of the people in all that they say to you," God advises the reluctant Samuel, his prophet and priest, whom the people have asked for a king. "It is not you they have rejected but me, not wishing me to reign over them anymore. They are now doing to you exactly what they have done to me since the day I brought them out of Egypt until now, deserting me and serving other gods."

God is prepared to accept a monarchy, provided the people understand what they are getting themselves into. Samuel gives the people YHWH's warnings: "This is what the king who is to reign over you will do. He will take your sons and direct them to his chariotry and cavalry, and they will run in front of his chariot. He will use them as leaders of a thousand and leaders of fifty; he will make them plough his fields and gather in his harvest and make his weapons of war and the gear for his chariots. He will take your daughters as perfumers, cooks, and bakers. He will take the best of your fields, your vineyards and your olive groves and give them to his officials. He will take the best of your servants, men and women, of your oxen and your donkeys, and make them work for him. He will tithe your flocks and you yourselves will become his slaves. When that day comes, you will cry aloud because of the king you have chosen for yourselves, but on that day YHWH will not hear you."

YHWH's percipient warnings, illuminating the unavoidable reality that when human beings invest one man with special power they simultaneously divest themselves, no longer resonate with the people. Because of their fear of the Philistines and other neighboring enemies they are willing to alter their constitution permanently. "No! We are determined to have a king," they cry, "so that we can be like other nations, with our own king to rule us and lead us and fight our battles."

YHWH's choice is Saul, "a handsome man in the prime of life," someone capable of symbolizing the people's aspirations. "Of all the Israelites there was no one more handsome than he," states the Book of Samuel. "He stood head and shoulders taller than anyone else." Samuel anoints Saul, who is confirmed by the whole people. The ceremony of divine anointing (or deputizing), followed by popular confirmation, will become the pattern for the Israelite monarchy. The anointing by a priest or prophet is meant to signify that this man is YHWH's choice, the confirmation by the assembly of the people that he is also the popular choice. In this way, Israel's new monarchic constitution is to retain a democratic aspect, suggestive of the medieval maxim *"Vox populi, vox Dei"* ("What the people approve, God approves"). This same procedure will be copied by the early church in its election of bishops (but because power adheres to the power-ful, confirmation by the people has fallen into disuse).

Saul proves himself an outstanding general, making war not only on the Philistines but on Moabites, Ammonites, Edomites, Amalekites, and all of Israel's neighboring ene-mies, for "whichever way he turned, he was victorious." But then Saul disobeys YHWH, first by offering sacrifice in Samuel's absence, then by sparing the Amalekite king and the most precious Amalekite booty from "the curse of de-struction"—that is, from universal extermination, one of YHWH's less pretty injunctions. There probably lies behind these stories a tug-of-war for ultimate power between the old prophet and the young king. But the upshot is that Saul loses the favor of YHWH, who "regrets having made Saul king."

Then YHWH says to Samuel, "Fill your horn with oil and go. I am sending you to Jesse of Bethlehem, for I have found myself a king from among his sons." At Bethlehem Samuel meets seven of Jesse's sons, but YHWH warns him to take no notice of their striking appearance or height, suggestive that they would all make fitting successors to Saul: "God does not see as human beings see; they look at appearances but YHWH looks at the heart."

"Are these all the sons you have?" asks Samuel of Jesse.

"There is still one left, the youngest; he is looking after the sheep."

"Send for him."

When the youngest arrives—barely beyond childhood but "ruddy, and withal of a beautiful countenance, and goodly to look to," according to King James—Samuel knows that this shepherd boy is God's unlikely choice. "At this, Samuel took the horn of oil and anointed him, surrounded by his brothers; and the spirit of YHWH seized on David from that day onwards."

Ruach YHWH—YHWH's spirit, or, more literally, his wind or breath—is as unpredictable as wind itself. On whom it will alight no one can say. And as with YHWH's other choices—of wily Avraham, dissembling Yaakov, tongue-tied Moshe, the carping Chosen People themselves—his election is always a surprise. But most surprising of all is what the man on whom this Spirit alights will have to say. The modern word *charisma,* taken from the Greek for "grace" or "divinely conferred gift," exactly describes what the Israelites expected from their leaders: a kind of inner glow, perceptible in a man's physical demeanor, that captures the observer's imagination and converts him to a partisan. But, more than his appearance, the charismatic's divine inspiration is proven by the words he speaks. In Israel's history, these words had always related to immediate need—as prophetic road maps to direct the people. Now, with the permanent settlement of the ex-nomads and the establishment of the monarchy, inspiration can take a new turn—as poetry.

Despairing Saul, who knows nothing of this second anointing but who imagines himself to have lost God's favor, sinks by degrees into madness. He calls for a musician to assuage his troubled spirit; and the musician drafted for this purpose is none other than David, the secret shepherd-king. Whenever "an evil spirit from YHWH afflicted [Saul] with terrors," David would be called to play his harp and sing his songs for the troubled king. "Saul would then be soothed; it would do him good and the evil spirit would leave him." David's music is completely lost; but his lyrics are still collected in the Book of Psalms, though we are no longer certain which psalms are David's and which were attributed to him over subsequent centuries.

Though David first achieves fame as a skilled harpist and poet—"the sweet singer of Israel," as later generations will call him—it is not long before he is tested on the field of battle. As Saul's earlier successes against the Philistines are gradually reversed, David's three eldest brothers are called to military service and find themselves in the Valley of the Terebinth in Judah, the Philistine battle line drawn up against them across the valley. At his father's behest, David comes loaded down with farm products—loaves of bread for his soldier brothers, rounds of cheese for their commanding officer—arriving on the scene just as the Philistine champion steps forth to issue a challenge to Israel. The man, named Goliath, is a giant who stands almost nine feet tall: "On his head was a bronze helmet and he wore a breastplate of scale-armor; the breastplate weighed five thousand shekels [about 125 pounds] of bronze. He had bronze greaves on his legs and a bronze scimitar slung across his shoulders. The shaft of his spear was like a weaver's beam, and the head of his spear weighed six hundred shekels [about 15 pounds] of iron." He shouts across the valley, "I challenge the ranks of Israel today. Give me a man and we will fight it out!" Single combat, instances of which we also find in the *Iliad,* was often used in ancient times to avoid the bloodletting of group combat—and to decide who would be subject to whom, as Goliath roars: "If he can fight it out with me and kill me, we will be your servants; but if I can beat him and kill him, you will become our servants and serve us."

Saul and "all Israel" are "dismayed and terrified." But David, learning that the man who slays Goliath will receive riches, the king's daughter, and exemption from all taxes (in that order), puts himself forward, declaring: "Who is this uncircumcised Philistine, to challenge the armies of the living God?" This sequence provides our first insight into David's character, bold, relying on God in all simplicity, but always with an eye to the main chance.

Saul, at first, will not allow such unequal combat: "You cannot go and fight the Philistine; you are only a boy and he has been a warrior since his youth." But as he listens to David's recital of his complete faith in YHWH, who enabled this shepherd boy to batter to death both lions and bears who attacked his sheep, he cannot help but be impressed. "YHWH," says David, "who delivered me from the claws of lion and bear, will deliver me from the clutches of this Philistine." Saul consents, even dressing David in the oppressive royal armor. "David tried to walk but not being used to them, said to Saul, 'I cannot walk in these; I am not used to them.'" So David is stripped and goes forth armed with only a sling and "five smooth stones"—and, like the wonder-boy of Michelangelo's statue, full of relaxed strength ready to spring.

Goliath laughs him to scorn, but David retorts: "You

come to me with sword, spear, and scimitar, but I come to you in the name of YHWH Sabaoth [the heavenly host or army], God of the armies of Israel, whom you have challenged. Today, YHWH will deliver you into my hand; I shall kill you, I shall cut off your head; today, I shall give your corpse and the corpses of the Philistine army to the birds of the air and the wild beasts, so that the whole world may know that there is a God in Israel, and this whole assembly know that YHWH does not give victory by means of sword and spear—for YHWH is lord of the battle and he will deliver you into our power."

This is a wonderful speech—and a wonderful moment in the history of Israel and of the human race—a resounding assertion that God is on the side of the small and powerless, not the high and mighty. This is a confrontation that has fixed itself permanently in human imagination; and who could count how many supposedly hopeless causes it has given strength and comfort to? There is every reason to presume that David, Israel's sweet singer, was capable of delivering such words. It is of a piece with his character as it will unfold throughout the historical Books of Samuel and Kings. With a wiliness more convoluted than Avraham's, a charm more compelling than Joseph's, a faith as deep as Moshe's, and a confidence all his own, this born politician, always playing to the crowd, captivates us as does no other figure in the whole of the Hebrew Bible.

Of course, he wins the day. The death of Goliath, felled by one well-directed stone to the forehead, panics the Philistine army, who are easily butchered in their flight. David, bearing Goliath's great head, returns in triumph with Saul. As the army marches along, "the women came out of all the towns of Israel singing and dancing to meet King Saul, with tambourines, sistrums and cries of joy; and as they danced the women sang:

"Saul has killed his thousands,
and David his tens of thousands."

Saul's angry reaction (especially in the King James Version) has the rhetorical quality of a Shakespearean soliloquy:

"They have ascribed unto David ten thousands,
and to me they have ascribed but thousands:
and what can he have more
but the kingdom?"

"And Saul," concludes the chronicler, "eyed David from that day and forward."

Saul offers David the hand of his daughter Merab in marriage, provided David "serve me bravely and fight YHWH's wars," but thinking to himself: "Better than strike the blow myself, let the Philistines do it!" David expresses reluctance, saying only: "Who am I in Israel, for me to become the king's son-in-law?" David, indeed, as a southerner, a member of the tribe of Judah, will need northern connections if he is ever to rule effectively—and Saul's Benjaminite family would be ideal in providing such. But before David can shed his ritual modesty, Saul humiliates him: "When the time came for Merab daughter of Saul to be given to David, she was given to Adriel of Meholah instead."

When Saul's second daughter, Michal, falls in love with David, he is ready to take advantage of the opportunity. But Saul proposes an odd exchange: "The king desires no bride-price except one hundred Philistine foreskins." Since it is a tricky business to take the foreskin of a man without his consent, Saul's proposal is meant to spell certain death for David. But David, rising to the challenge, thinks "it would be a fine thing to be the king's son-in-law. And no time was lost before David got up to go," returning in record time with *two* hundred Philistine foreskins, which he counts out before the king. By this savagely hilarious feat, David endears himself to the Israelites even more than by the slaying of Goliath.

But having humiliated the king, called his bluff, and married his daughter in the bargain, David has put himself in greater danger, for "Saul could not but see that YHWH was with David, and that the whole House of Israel loved him. Saul, more afraid of David than ever, became his inveterate enemy. The Philistine chiefs kept mounting their campaigns but, whenever they did so, David proved more successful than any of Saul's staff; consequently he gained great re-nown."

David, loved by all, is oblivious of the king's resentment. But among his most fervent admirers is Saul's son Jonathan, who "delighted much in David" and who tips him off to the royal plans for David's assassination—as does Michal, who saves his life by placing a life-sized idol under the cover of David's bed while he escapes. David, now in full flight before the king's wrath, stays briefly with a Philistine king, who also grows to resent him for his prowess. David's ploy for escaping the jealousy of *this* king is to feign a madness reminiscent of Hamlet's, till the exasperated king kicks him out: "Have I not enough madmen, without your bringing me this one to weary me with his antics?"

David the outlaw comes to live among the outlaws of the Judean hill country, gradually building up a band of cutthroat mercenaries, fiercely loyal comrades who will one day become the nucleus of King David's enormous personal bodyguard—an essential element in his later political success. Meanwhile, David has become an obsession with Saul, who sends his men to hunt David down—and even sets out on the hunt himself. During the course of one of these hunting parties, Saul, who has three thousand men scouring the desert of En-gedi, finds himself impelled to relieve nature and, spotting a cave along the route, enters it alone "to cover his feet," as the Bible euphemistically puts it—that is, to let his loincloth drop around his ankles while he squats down in the cave.

And who should be occupying the recesses of the cave at that very moment but David and his merry men. David creeps up on Saul, intending to kill him, but at the last stays his hand and silently cuts off the border of Saul's cloak, which the king had taken off and hung on an outcrop. After Saul has finished the royal business and left the cave, David leaves too, calling after the king: "My lord king!" Saul swerves around, astonished to see his prey bowing to the ground like any obedient subject.

David then declaims across the desert distance between them: "Why do you listen to people who say, 'David intends your ruin'? This very day you have seen for yourself how YHWH put you in my power in the cave and how, refusing to kill you, I spared you saying, 'I will not raise my hand against my lord, since he is YHWH's anointed.' Look, father, look at the border of your cloak in my hand. Since, although I cut the border off your cloak, I did not kill you, surely you realize that I intend neither mischief nor crime. I have not wronged you, and yet you hunt me down to take my life. May YHWH be judge between me and you, and may YHWH avenge me on you; but I shall never lay a hand on you!"

Another eloquent speech from a master wordsmith, who, though he may be canny enough to appreciate that his refusal to lay a hand on the present king may have most positive implications for the *next* king, seems unable to believe that anyone could actually dislike him, David, the wonder-boy. This young man's sense of entitlement long preceded his anointing.

At David's sudden appearance and startling speech, Saul, already unhinged, becomes incoherent, weeping loudly and calling David his son: "You are upright and I am not! . . . Now I know that you will indeed reign and that the sovereignty of Israel will pass into your hands." He begs David not to kill his family or blot out his name "once I am gone"; and then he goes "home while David and his men went back to the stronghold." For all its emotion, this is not a reconciliation scene; and the evidence for what happens next is equivocal. There is a second story of David's sparing Saul, which is probably just a tamer, alternative account of the cave episode, but which the scrupulous chronicler could not bring himself to omit. Then David, who despite Saul's hysterical confession does not feel it safe to go home, finds himself a job as vassal warlord to the Philistines. He has also picked up two new wives along the way—Ahinoam of Jezreel (of whom we are told nothing) and Abigail, "a woman of intelligence and beauty" whose rare pluck, generosity, and wisdom saved David and his men from hunger and brought her to the attention of this warrior chieftain, who never fails to respond to feminine beauty. Before David can consummate their union, her inconvenient husband, a churl named Nabal (whose name in Hebrew means something like "brutal fool"), providentially dies from fear of David, who never touches him. Michal, David's first wife, we learn at this point, has been given to a new husband by the vengeful Saul.

David's position as vassal to Israel's enemies the Philistines is a most uncomfortable one, but it is hard to imagine how he could have survived without such protection; and, in any case, he uses his position to overcome such tribes as the Geshurites, the Girzites, and the Amalekites, who are at least as noisome to the Israelites as they are to the Philistines. When at last the Philistines muster all their forces for a final attack on Saul's now-weakened kingdom, the desperate king consults a medium in order to raise the ghost of the recently dead Samuel, who tells Saul that all is lost and that "tomorrow you and your sons will be with me." Luckily for David, the confederation of Philistine chieftains rejects his participation in the battle, "in case he turns on us once battle is joined. Would there be a better way for the man to regain his master's favor than with the heads of these men here?" David, who has been pretending to be eager for Israelite blood, is secretly relieved. He could never have fought his countrymen.

The Israelites are routed at Mount Gilboa; and both Saul and Jonathan, David's loving friend, die in the battle. The Book of Samuel records David's lament on hearing this news, in words that are almost certainly authentic, magnanimous in victory, respectful of the kingship, and full of the camaraderie of Bronze Age and Iron Age warriors, who valued the fellowship of men far above the love of women. David's description of his love for Jonathan is virtually a direct quotation from Gilgamesh's lament for Enkidu:

"The beauty of Israel is slain
upon thy high places:
how are the mighty fallen!

"Tell it not in Gath,
publish it not in the streets of Askelon;
lest the daughters of the Philistines rejoice,
lest the daughters of the uncircumcised triumph.

"Ye mountains of Gilboa,
let there be no dew,
neither let there be rain, upon you, nor fields of offerings;
for there the shield of the mighty is vilely cast away,
the shield of Saul,
as though he had not been anointed with oil.

"From the blood of the slain,
from the fat of the mighty,
the bow of Jonathan turned not back,
and the sword of Saul returned not empty.

"Saul and Jonathan were lovely and pleasant in their lives;
and in their death they were not divided;
they were swifter than eagles,
they were stronger than lions.

"Ye daughters of Israel, weep over Saul,
who clothed you in scarlet, with other delights,
who put on ornaments of gold
upon your apparel.

"How are the mighty fallen
in the midst of battle!

"O Jonathan,
thou wast slain in thine high places.
I am distressed for thee, my brother Jonathan:

very pleasant hast thou been unto me:
thy love to me was wonderful,
passing the love of women.

"How are the mighty fallen,
and the weapons of war perished!"

David is publicly consecrated king at Hebron, where the bodies of his Abrahamic ancestors lie and which now becomes the capital of the southern kingdom, for he is, as yet, acknowledged only by his own people—by Judah. A war ensues between the northerners and southerners—between the House of Saul and the House of David—but it is not long before the northern kingdom of Israel capitulates and David is anointed once more at Hebron, this time with the warrior nobles of the north in attendance. The politically astute king, now but thirty years old, realizes that Hebron, deep in southern territory, will not do as capital of the United Kingdom of Israel. He marches on the Jebusite town of Jerusalem, an enclave between north and south—and a capital that will suit his purposes admirably. He captures the town, also known as the "citadel of Zion," strategically situated on a hill and ever after called the "City of David." He meets a final Philistine attack, and victory again is swift. David is now the unchallenged ruler of Canaan, a land which can for the first time be called Israel and which will soon stretch south into the Sinai and north to the Lebanese mountains, west to the Mediterranean (along a part of which the defeated Philistines are contained in a narrow coastal

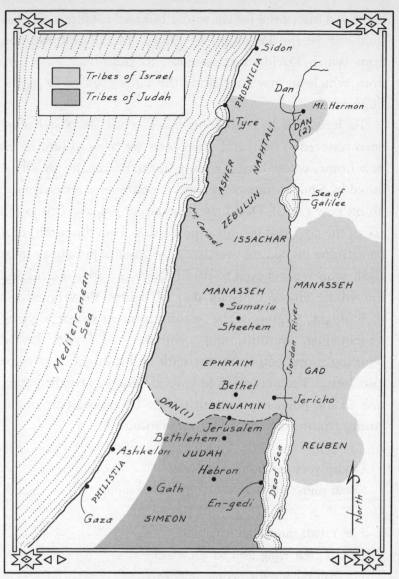

THE UNITED KINGDOM OF ISRAEL

Noted are the approximate areas of settlement of the Twelve Tribes, as well as the border between the ten tribes of Israel and the two tribes of Judah.

strip) and east of the Jordan to the borders of Gilead. Farther southeast lie the kingdoms of Edom, Moab, and Ammon from which David exacts tribute; to the northeast Aram, from which he may have done the same even as far as the Euphrates.

To Jerusalem he brings his three wives, Michal having been restored to him, and many sons are born to him in his new home, where David, adding to the harem already established by Saul, acquires wives and concubines at a steady rate. To his new capital, David, ever the astute pol, also brings the ark of the covenant in a great procession from the south, thus confirming his control over Israel by physical proximity to its God, who was believed to dwell above the ark. "David and the whole House of Israel danced before YHWH with all their might, singing to the accompaniment of harps, lyres, tambourines, sistrums, and cymbals. . . . David danced whirling round before YHWH with all his might, wearing a loincloth." The music would have included a Davidic psalm, one of the popular poems that were becoming part of the young conqueror's escalating reputation:

O clap your hands, all ye people;
Shout unto God with the voice of triumph!

For YHWH most high is terrible;
he is a great King over all the earth.
He shall subdue the people under us,
and the nations under our feet.

He shall choose our inheritance for us,
the excellency of Yaakov whom he loved.

God is gone up with a shout,
YHWH with the sound of a trumpet!

Sing praises to God, sing praises;
sing praises unto our King, sing praises!

For God is the King of all the earth:
sing ye praises with understanding.
God reigneth over the heathen:
God sitteth upon the throne of his holiness.

The princes of the people are gathered together,
even the people of the God of Avraham;
for the shields of the earth belong unto God:
he is greatly exalted!

The new king, at the acme of his vigor and enjoying his triumph to the hilt, must have presented a thrilling sight to his people. But not to Michal, the twice-traded wife, herself the daughter of a king but now just an elder member of the expanding harem. "When she saw King David leaping and whirling round before YHWH, the sight of him filled her with contempt. They brought the ark of YHWH in and put it in position, inside the tent which David had erected for it; and David presented burnt offerings and communion sacrifices in YHWH's presence. And when David had finished presenting burnt offerings, he blessed the people in the name of YHWH Sabaoth. To all the people, to the whole multitude of Israelites, men and women, he then distributed to each a loaf of bread, a portion of meat and a raisin cake."

As David returns to bless his own household, Michal steps forward:

"Much honor the king of Israel has won today, making an exhibition of himself under the eyes of his servant-maids, making an exhibition of himself like a buffoon!"

"I was dancing for YHWH, not for them. As YHWH lives, who chose me in preference to your father and his whole family to make me leader of Israel, YHWH's people, I shall dance before YHWH and lower myself even further than that. In your eyes I may be base, but by the maids you speak of, by them, I shall be held in honor."

This sour exchange is full of the resonance of real life. David's endless vitality and enthusiasm are the very qualities that have endeared him to the common people. He knows it, basks in their love, and returns their ardor. Though he is quite happy with himself, he is humble in his way, crediting God with everything. But a man who loves a crowd is seldom as effective in intimate relationships as he is in the midst of the throng. The histories of politics, sports, and entertainment are replete with such figures, triumphant in public, tragic in private.

———

David will dote on his sons, spoiled brats brought up in uncommon luxury, not the stuff of which warrior-kings are made. One of them, his beloved Absalom, will try to usurp the kingship, wooing the northern nobles to his cause and to a bloody battle in the Forest of Ephraim between David's immense personal guard and an easily routed army of northerners. Absalom's undignified demise in the course of battle leaves David a broken man, beset by political dissensions that threaten the future of the United Kingdom. David's inconsolable grief for this unworthy son is one of the most touching scenes in the whole of the Bible, as the king wanders from room to room, repeating over and over, "Oh, my son Absalom! My son! My son Absalom! If only I had died instead of you! Oh, Absalom my son, my son!"

But long before this happens, David engages in another sortie that can hardly have made for domestic peace. It was spring, the chronicler tells us, "the time when kings go campaigning." Something, however, has kept the king in Jerusalem—business, weariness, complacency?—while his soldiers have gone off on the proper business of massacring Ammonites. The restless monarch is pacing back and forth on the palace roof when he sees a woman bathing, and "the woman was very beautiful." He makes inquiries and learns that she is Bathsheba, the wife of Uriah the Hittite, a member of the king's guard, just now off campaigning against the Ammonites. David sends for Bathsheba. Then, in terse recital, the chronicler tells us: "She came to him, and he lay with her, just after she had purified herself from her period. She then went home again. The woman conceived and sent word to David, 'I am pregnant.' " In short order, David arranges to have Uriah sent to the front lines of the battle and the rest of the men fall back, so that Uriah is killed. The moment Bathsheba's mourning is over, David sends for her: "She became his wife and bore him a son. But what David had done displeased YHWH."

Enter the prophet Nathan to tell the king a story:

"In the same town were two men,
one rich, the other poor.
The rich man had flocks and herds
in great abundance;
the poor man had nothing but a ewe lamb,
only a single little one which he had bought.
He fostered it and it grew up with him and his children,
eating his bread, drinking from his cup,
sleeping in his arms; it was like a daughter to him.
When a traveler came to stay, the rich man
would not take anything from his own flock or herd
to provide for the wayfarer who had come to him.
Instead, he stole the poor man's lamb
and prepared that for his guest."

Hearing this, David flew into "a great rage," demanding to know who the man was who did this "thing without pity."

"You are the man. YHWH, God of Israel, says this, 'I

anointed you king of Israel, I saved you from Saul's clutches, I gave you your master's household and your master's wives into your arms, I gave you the House of Israel and the House of Judah; and, if this is too little, I shall give you other things as well. Why did you show contempt for YHWH, by doing what displeases him?"

One can only cringe before the accusation, which is exactly what David does. "I have sinned against YHWH," he admits immediately. Even at his worst, David's spontaneous honesty makes him lovable. One of life's recurring sufferings surely derives from the chronic inability of human beings to own up to what they have done, but David's grief for his sins is as genuine as any in the long history of contrition:

> "Have mercy upon me, O God, according to thy
>   lovingkindness:
> according unto the multitude of thy tender mercies blot out
>   my transgressions.
> Wash me thoroughly from mine iniquity,
> and cleanse me from my sin.
>
> "For I acknowledge my transgressions:
> and my sin is ever before me.
> Against thee, thee only, have I sinned,
> and done this evil in thy sight:
>
> "that thou mightest be justified when thou speakest,
> and be clear when thou judgest.

Behold, I was shapen in iniquity;
and in sin did my mother conceive me."✶

"Behold thou desirest truth in the inward parts:
and in the hidden part thou shalt make me to know
    wisdom.
Purge me with hyssop, and I shall be clean:
wash me, and I shall be whiter than snow.

"Make me to hear joy and gladness;
that the bones which thou hast broken may rejoice.
Hide thy face from my sins,
and blot out all mine iniquities.

"Create in me a clean heart, O God;
and renew a right spirit within me.
Cast me not away from thy presence;
and take not thy holy spirit from me.

✶ This line is one of the sources for Augustine of Hippo's doctrine of original sin, incurred by Adam and Eve in Eden and passed to all subsequent generations by sexual intercourse. *Pace* Augustine, the line does not mean that David's mother committed sin by conceiving him through sexual intercourse. It is just an instance of the common ancient assumption that human beings are evil. See the words of Ut-napishtim et al., page 61; also the words of Jesus in Matthew 7:11.

"Restore unto me the joy of thy
    salvation;
and uphold me with thy free spirit.
. . . .
O Lord, open thou my lips;
and my mouth shall shew forth thy
    praise.

"For thou desirest not sacrifice;
    else would I give it:

thou delightest not in burnt offering.

The sacrifices of God are a broken spirit:

a broken and a contrite heart, O God, thou wilt not
    despise."

David is no visionary. When he "consults" YHWH, he does so by casting pebbles drawn from the *ephod,* using a method not unlike that of the Ouija board, or he listens to prophets like Samuel and Nathan. For all his anointings, he is not a religious leader but a political one; and from this time on, the leadership that was once embodied in a single prophet like Moshe will be divided between prophets, acknowledged men of God, and kings, taken up with more secular concerns. Even David's "inspiration," poured forth in his Psalms, is of a more earthly variety than the Voice that spoke to Avraham and Moshe. For David is not the mouthpiece of YHWH but a man on his knees or a devotee dancing in a public procession. One reason that he has always captivated readers of the Bible is that he is closer to our own experience than are the solitary prophets. He is the captain of the football team, the supersalesman, the engaging entertainer, the charismatic politician. We know the man.

The journey through the wilderness is being gradually transformed into a journey to the unknown recesses of the self—to "the inward parts." This new spiritual journey will prove as eventful and unpredictable as the physical one, full of pitfalls and surprises. God forgives David; but there are consequences for the king, whose household, as Nathan prophesies, "will never be free of the sword" and whose wives will be given "to your neighbor"—Absalom, as it turns out, who during his rebellion will need to assert his royal prerogatives—"who will lie with your wives in broad daylight."

There is through all the biblical writings we have considered thus far an assumption that whoever obeys YHWH will be rewarded with prosperity and long life, and whoever does not will be punished with suffering and death. Saul's case is especially instructive in this regard. Because he lost the kingship, succeeding generations had to find something he did wrong, since his failure could be accounted for only by YHWH's abandonment of the king, which in turn could be accounted for only by some royal transgression. What they came up with—two ritual sins—are pretty lame excuses for YHWH's wrath. David's sins—adulterous theft and the vindictive murder of an innocent commoner—should be far more consequential, but since David died a natural death in old age, the only important *political* consequence that could be discovered for his sins was Absalom's rebellion. This harsh outlook, that worldly success and prosperity are certain indicators of God's favor—long before the Calvinism with which it is usually associated—must leave both mind and heart unsatisfied and will gradually be revised as the biblical journey is transformed from a physical adventure to a spiritual one. As the Israelites look more deeply into their "hidden part," the crudeness of this tit-for-tat morality will become more obvious to them.

But it is with David that the interior journey begins. A sense of the self is notably absent in all ancient literatures. *I,* as we commonly use it today to mean one's interior self, is seldom in evidence before the humanist autobiographies of the early modern period (such as *The Autobiography of Benvenuto Cellini*). Before these, we can count only a few instances from earlier literatures: *The Confessions* of Augustine of Hippo in the fifth century A.D., some fragments from the sixth century B.C. attributed to Sappho, and—oldest of all—the Psalms, which are filled with *I*'s: the *I* of repentance, the *I* of anger and vengeance, the *I* of self-pity and self-doubt, the *I* of despair, the *I* of delight, the *I* of ecstasy. The Psalms, some of which were undoubtedly written in the tenth century by David himself, are a treasure trove of personal emotions from poets acutely attuned to their inner states, from ancient harpists dramatically aware that spirit calls to Spirit— that their pain and joy can find permanent satisfaction only in the Creator of all: "When I consider thy heavens, the work of thy fingers, the moon and the stars, which thou hast ordained; . . . keep me as the apple of the eye, hide me under the shadow of thy wings. . . . O taste and see that YHWH is good. . . . My heart was hot within me, while I was musing the fire burned. . . . My God, my God, why hast thou forsaken me? why art thou so far from helping me, and from the words of my roaring? . . . For I am a stranger with thee, and a sojourner, as all my fathers were. . . . As the hart panteth after the water brooks, so panteth my soul after thee, O God. . . ." "Be still, and know that I am God."

In this bubbling spring of self-reflection, this unparalleled resource of prayer drawn on repeatedly by Jews and Christians over the millennia, there is no poem more cherished than the Psalm of the Good Shepherd, the world's favorite prayer:

> The LORD is my shepherd; I shall not want.
> He maketh me to lie down in green pastures;
> he leadeth me beside the still waters.
> He restoreth my soul:
> he leadeth me in the paths of righteousness
> for his name's sake.
>
> Yea, though I walk through the valley of the shadow of
>   death,
> I will fear no evil: for thou art with me;
> thy rod and thy staff they comfort me.
>
> Thou preparest a table before me
> in the presence of mine enemies:
> thou anointest my head with oil;
> my cup runneth over.
>
> Surely goodness and mercy shall follow me
> all the days of my life:
> and I will dwell in the house of the LORD
> for ever.

This song of trust, this affecting attitude of childlike confidence in God, must be the work of the great shepherd-king, who danced naked "only for YHWH" and was not ashamed to humble himself before his people. David may share some attitudes with the warrior-kings of Sumer, but they would only have been, like Michal, appalled at his willingness to play God's fool, a king who always retained something of the playful humor of the shepherd boy who counted out the Philistine foreskins, who played the madman in Philistia, who watched the squatting monarch with twinkling amusement.

David remains always God's little fighter, exhibiting the same scrappy confidence he showed when he stood up to the giant before all Israel. In Jerusalem today, as a pilgrim approaches the ramparts of the Old City, one can almost imagine that David still stands upon his great conquest, his citadel of Zion, easy, confident, his tight muscles rippling as he laughs, shaking his head in disbelief that the City of David, so often razed, has grown so huge. In his day it occupied one hill, its roofs could be counted from afar, and it housed scarcely more than two thousand souls. But it is still there; and its continued existence brings us back to its royal founder, the little king of the little city, and the God he served—

Holy Zion's help forever,
And her confidence alone.

SIX

BABYLON

✳

From Many to One

Despite the amorous exploits recorded in the Book of Samuel, David must be considered a sexual moderate among ancient monarchs. His son and successor Solomon, installed on the throne after some behind-the-scenes string-pulling by his mother, Bathsheba, and the prophet Nathan, quickly expanded the royal harem to seven hundred wives and three hundred concubines, contributing considerably to the population boom in Jerusalem, which soon spread out over the neighboring hillside. Solomon's appetites were hardly confined to the harem. In fact, the acquisition of new wives was principally for political, rather than sexual, gratification. Each new acquisition was made to further an alliance, none more important than the one brought about by Solomon's acquisition of Pharaoh's daughter, for whom he built a separate palace on the new hill to the north.

Since Solomon's father had vanquished the Philistines, who had been the only credible threat to Israelite suzerainty over the Levant, and since the Davidic kingdom had reached almost to the borders of Egypt in the south, Syria in the north, and Mesopotamia in the east, Solomon was in the enviable position of being the middleman between fabulously wealthy societies. Israel was the necessary trade route for all caravans—and, as any businessman will tell you, if your choice is between being a producer of goods or a middleman who takes a percentage, the sure bet is to take the percentage. No startup costs, no ongoing production costs, no overhead, no inventory, no insurance, just the expense of collecting the toll.

His treasury overflowing, Solomon embarked on a building program the likes of which the land of Canaan had never seen, an enterprise of such ambition as to rival the fabled civilizations that lay at his distant borders. Gold, silver, bronze, and iron, cloths of scarlet, crimson, and violet, scented wood from Ophir, and Lebanese trunks of cedar and juniper all poured into Jerusalem, along with architects and designers, engravers and carpenters, and skilled workers of all kinds. "All King Solomon's drinking vessels were of gold, and all the plate in the House of the Forest of Lebanon was of pure gold; silver was little thought of in Solomon's days, since the king had a fleet of Tarshish at sea . . . and once every three years the fleet of Tarshish would come back laden with gold and silver, ivory, apes, and baboons. For riches and for wisdom, King Solomon surpassed all kings on earth, and the whole world consulted Solomon to hear the wisdom which God had implanted in his heart; and everyone would bring a present with him: things made of silver, things made of gold, robes, armor, spices, horses, and mules; and this went on year after year."

And though this goes on page after page, I will not inflict it on you further. How wise was Solomon anyway, and how much was his reputation based on wealth alone? Solomon was certainly not wise in the mess he left behind him.

At first, his unskilled workers were defeated Canaanites impressed into service. But once the Egyptian princess's palace was built, and the king's palace, which covered the whole crest of the new hill, and, adjacent to it, the Temple of YHWH—a new house for the ark grander even than the storied temples of Egypt and Babylon—Solomon's designs grew ever more elaborate. He needed roads, he needed bridges, he needed to fortify his defenses throughout the realm, he needed special "chariot cities" to hold his cavalry, he needed . . . storage cities such as the pharaohs had built with impressed Israelite labor. He began to impress Israelites; and, since his treasury was now empty, he began to tax exorbitantly—the surest way in the world to lose the affection of one's subjects.

Solomon was succeeded by his son Rehoboam, the third member of the House of David to sit on the throne of Israel. As so often happens, the creative energy of the founder was followed by the presumption of the second generation—and then by the presumption and stupidity of the third. By the time of Rehoboam's enthronement, the strains in the union had reached such a crisis that the nobles of the northern tribes delivered a threat: "Your father laid a cruel yoke on us; if you will lighten your father's cruel slavery, that heavy yoke which he imposed on us, we are willing to serve you." Strapping young Rehoboam, taken aback, temporizes, asking for "three days' time." His elders advise him that "if you are kind to these people, pleasant to them, and give them a fair reply, they will remain your servants forever." But not wishing to commence his reign with a show of weakness, he rejects this advice and consults his buddies, "the young men who had grown up with him," who urge him to hold the line. When the northern nobles return in three days for the king's response, he gives them a little speech, concocted for him by his buds: "My dick is fatter than my father's thigh! So—my father laid a heavy yoke on you? Mine will be even heavier! My father kept you in line with the lash? I'll whip you with scorpions!" Way to go, Rehoboam!

Thus dies the United Kingdom of Israel. Henceforth the northern kingdom will go its own way under its own king.

In three generations the House of David went from exaltation among the nations to unrivaled prosperity to the disaster of a rump state, the Kingdom of Judah. But in that brief time, Hebrew literature was born—in a language that was but a slight variant of the common language of Canaan and using the world's first alphabet, invented by Israel's northern neighbors, the Semites of Phoenicia. David's Psalms were followed, during Solomon's reign, with the writing down of the ancient stories. This record was later entwined with stories from the north (often the same stories differently told) and still later emended and refined to fit the agendas of priests and monarchs, giving us the Torah as we have it today.

In addition to the early monarchy's matchless contribution of early Hebrew literature, the United Kingdom of Israel lasted just long enough to establish in the mind of people north and south the idea that monarchical government was their natural destiny; and monarchical leadership will perdure till the fall of both kingdoms. But the procession of kings that will sit on the thrones of Saul and David over the centuries to come will seldom measure up to expectations, normally exhibiting Saul's vacillations or Solomon's cruelties or undesirable qualities all their own, till there will rise in the hearts of their subjects a sharp longing for the return of the true king, a second David; and the myth of the Kingdom of David will grow to Arthurian proportions, transformed over time into an ever more detailed belief that one day God will send another messiah, a divinely "anointed one," his true deputy come at last to save his people.

But long before such daydreaming commences, the notion of an inspired leader, like Moshe, whom God used as a medium to speak to the people, will recede into the distant past, a part of the narrative of the ancestors; and the king will become just another figure of political power, often unreasonable, sometimes tyrannical, with nothing special to say. Thanks to David's establishment of the cult of YHWH in Jerusalem and Solomon's uniting of cult and monarchy in a great building complex beetling over Jerusalem, even the priests of YHWH will become but temple functionaries, members of the monarchical establishment, little more than bureaucrats, more like the priest-politicians of Egypt and Mesopotamia than like the Hebrew priest-prophets of former times. One can no longer expect from them the kind of prophetic insight that Samuel brought to the inventive task of creating the monarchy or that Nathan brought to the daunting task of admonishing the king. We are back to the old problem of who will be God's mouthpiece: who is open enough to hear God's word and courageous enough to speak it aloud? Certainly not the officially anointed king or the officially appointed priests. What is needed is someone *unofficial*, a radical outsider.

In the northern kingdom, the new king wastes no time in setting up a cult to rival Jerusalem's, an altar at Bethel for *two* golden calves—"gods that are no gods," in the opinion of Judah. In the second quarter of the ninth century B.C. there comes to the throne of Israel Ahab and his powerful Phoenician queen Jezebel, whom the Book of Kings portrays as a painted harlot. She is a zealous worshiper of Baal and high priestess of Baal's Asherah, and the Bible depicts her as a sort of Canaanite Lady Macbeth. Ahab builds a temple to Baal in his northern capital of Samaria, sacrificing two of his sons in the process, while Jezebel occupies herself "butchering the prophets of YHWH," probably bands of roving ecstatics.

Elijah the Tishbite, the last prophet left, challenges the prophets of Baal to a dramatic duel on the slopes of Mount Carmel: each side will offer sacrifice and the one whose sacrifice is consumed by fire from heaven will win—and his god will be acknowledged as the true god by the people. The results are predictable; in fact, the whole narrative of Elijah, which is full of vindictive miracles and ends with the prophet being taken up to heaven in a fiery chariot, has a kind of naive conventionality to it, except for one incident which takes place in Sinai on the "Mountain of God," where Elijah has sought temporary refuge.

"There he went into a cave and spent the night there. Then the word of YHWH came to him saying, 'What are you doing here, Elijah?' He replied, 'I am full of jealous zeal for

YHWH Sabaoth, because the Israelites have abandoned your covenant, have torn down your altars, and put your prophets to the sword. I am the only one left, and now they want to kill me. Then he was told, 'Go out and stand on the mountain before YHWH.' At that moment YHWH was going by. A mighty hurricane split the mountains and shattered the rocks before YHWH. But YHWH was not in the hurricane. And after the hurricane, an earthquake. But YHWH was not in the earthquake. And after the earthquake, fire. But YHWH was not in the fire. And after the fire, a light murmuring sound"—which in King James is beautifully rendered as "a still, small voice."

YHWH is not Baal the bull, not a storm god, after all. He controls the weather, since he is its Creator, but he is not *in* any of its elements; he does not belong to the special effects. He is in us, the still, small voice, the murmuring of personal conscience. For once, we are given a description of the Voice that has played the central role in all our narratives, and it sounds quite other than what we might expect. Elijah is a prophet in the old style: like Samuel, he belongs to a priestly brotherhood and his revelations are private oracles for the king. But in this one episode he gives us something new and provides a kind of bridge to what will happen next.

About the middle of the eighth century, a Judean shepherd named Amos, living a few miles outside Bethlehem, is seized by a message from God and impelled to head north to preach to idolatrous Israel, which is enjoying high-flying economic success, a success that has passed some of its population by. Amos is decidedly not a professional prophet, like

Elijah, and has no connection with any of the prophetic brotherhoods. He is, in his own words, "merely a herdsman and dresser of sycamore-figs," as is evident from his rough, prickly words, delivered at the schismatic shrine of Bethel and in the streets of Samaria. There the shocked shepherd is witness to conspicuous consumption on a grand scale, which he realizes is just a new form of social injustice:

"Listen to this, you cows of Bashan
living on the hill of Samaria [the best real estate],
exploiting the weak and ill-treating the poor,
saying to your husbands, 'Bring us something to drink!'
The Lord God has sworn by his holiness:
'Look, the days will soon be on you
when he will use hooks to drag you away
and fish-hooks for the very last of you;
through the breaches in the wall you will leave,
each one straight ahead,
and be herded away towards Hermon,'
declares YHWH."

The leisurely ladies of Samaria were not used to being addressed in this manner, nor were their prosperous husbands, whom Amos accuses thus:

" 'They hate the man who teaches justice at the city gate
and detest anyone who declares the truth.
For trampling on the poor man
and for extorting levies on his wheat:

although you have built houses of dressed stone,
you will never live in them;
although you have planted pleasant vineyards,
you will not drink wine from them:
for I know how many your crimes are
and how outrageous your sins,
you oppressors of the upright, who hold people to ransom
and thrust the poor aside at the gates. . . .'

"Seek good and not evil
so that you may survive,
and YHWH Sabaoth, be with you
as you claim he is.
Hate evil, love good.
let justice reign at the city gate."

The growing revulsion of the people of Israel against this
loud nuisance in their streets is only increased when he dares
criticize—in God's name—their elegant piety:

" 'I hate, I scorn your festivals,
I take no pleasure in your solemn assemblies.
When you bring me burnt offerings . . .
your oblations, I do not accept them
and I do not look at your communion sacrifices of fat cattle.
Spare me the din of your chanting,
let me hear none of your strumming on lyres,
but let justice flow like water,
and uprightness like a never-failing stream.' "

It was an amazing performance, the more so that it was completely unexpected—and Amos got himself expelled from Israel in short order. But during his brief celebrity, he had taken the old art of prophecy and shaped it into a new instrument for a new age. Long gone were the popular leaders like Moshe, acknowledged by all, long gone the good kings like David, gone the priests like Samuel and the prophets like Nathan who spoke truth to power. So God raised up a nobody from nowhere to tell the truth—openly, without riddles, and in everyone's hearing—a shepherd with the smell of the pasture still on him, bellowing out the truth to the smug and perfumed.

And the truth—for eighth-century Samaria—was this: to serve God means to act with justice. One cannot pray and offer sacrifice while ignoring the poor, the beggars at the gates. But more radical still: if you have more than you need, you are a thief, for what you "own" is stolen from those who do not have enough. You are a murderer, who lives on the abundance that has been taken from the mouths of the starving. You are an idolater, for what you worship is not the true God. You are a whore, for you have bedded down with other gods, the gods of your own comfort and self-delusion, you who "cram [your] palaces with violence and extortion," who have "sold the upright for silver and the poor for a pair of sandals [from Gucci, no doubt]," who "have crushed the heads of the weak into the dust and thrust the rights of the oppressed to one side."

Amos is joined by a younger contemporary, Hosea, who preaches in a similar style, but who, because of his own experience with an unfaithful wife, is able to enrich his preaching with the dramatic metaphor of Israel as the whoring wife of a loving God. Hosea's yearning for Gomer, his wife, is painfully unrequited—and so mixed up with God's love for Israel that it is not always possible to distinguish the reality from the metaphor:

> But look, I am going to seduce her
> and lead her into the desert
> and speak to her heart. . . .
> There she will respond to me as when she was young,
> as on the day when she came up from Egypt.

Thus the metaphor of a courtship and "holy marriage" between Israel and God, first broached in the desert narrative of Exodus, is given a new twist. But both Amos and Hosea also look forward to a "Day of YHWH," a terrible day of vengeance in which the exploiters will receive their justice and, according to Amos, only a "remnant" will be saved. The images of the Day and the remnant, met here for the first time, will come to be of increasing importance as the new prophetic movement grows in strength.

In 721, the Day of YHWH arrived for the Kingdom of Israel, which had recently been reduced to the status of a vassal kingdom by the expanding Assyrian empire to the northeast. But soon after the death of Tiglath-pileser III, Assyria's great warrior emperor, Israel decided to flex its muscles and throw off the Assyrian yoke. This was its last mistake. The Assyrians descended and carried off all the people of property, dispersing Israelite nobles throughout the empire as nameless slaves who would never be heard from again. In time to come, their land would be colonized by subject peoples from elsewhere in the empire, who one day, intermarried with the remaining peasant stock, would come to be known as Samaritans.

Amos knew what he was talking about. He even had right the direction of this permanent exile—northeast "toward Hermon," as he had warned the "cows of Bashan," now deprived of their homes and finery and even their identities. As a people, Israel had simply evaporated—ten Lost Tribes,* who leave no further trace in the historical record.

W e do not know how this horrific confirmation of Amos's and Hosea's prophecies was understood by the remaining Children of the Promise—the Judeans of the southern kingdom, the people who would soon be known as the Jews—now "the remnant" prophesied by Amos. But the people of the south had their own new prophets; and preeminent among these gadflies stood the man who is perhaps the greatest of all prophets, Isaiah of Judah. Quite unlike Amos, Isaiah was an educated man with access to kings and may even have been a writer—the first literary prophet, though the less than seamless quality of the Book

---

* The Ten Tribes of Israel are (from north to south) Dan, Naphtali, Asher, Zebulun, Issachar, Joseph (subdivided into the tribes of Manasseh and Ephraim); Gad and Reuben (in Transjordan); and Benjamin (just north of the border with Judah)—all of whom made up the Kingdom of Israel. The tribes remaining are Judah and Simeon, who make up the southern Kingdom of Judah.

of Isaiah suggests that his oracles were arranged by his disciples after his death.

When Isaiah was twenty-five, he had a vision in Solomon's Temple at Jerusalem of God enthroned in his heavenly sanctuary, surrounded by seraphim, the six-winged "fiery ones," who shout

"Holy, holy, holy
YHWH Sabaoth.
All the earth is full of his glory."

Isaiah, whose lips are purified with a fiery coal by one of the seraphs, is then sent forth to tell the truth, which no one will believe, "until towns are in ruins and deserted, houses untenanted and a great desolation reigns in the land, and YHWH has driven the people away and the country is totally abandoned."

Isaiah's first prophecies have all the well-wrought balance of literature:

My beloved had a vineyard
on a fertile hillside.
He dug it, cleared it of stones,
and planted it with red grapes.
In the middle he built a tower,
he hewed a press there too.
He expected it to yield fine grapes:
wild grapes were all it yielded.

"And now, citizens of Jerusalem and people of Judah,
I ask you to judge between me and my vineyard.
What more could I have done for my vineyard
that I have not done?
Why, when I expected it to yield fine grapes,
has it yielded wild ones?

"Very well, I shall tell you what I am going to do to my
    vineyard:
I shall take away its hedge, for it to be grazed on,
and knock down its wall, for it to be trampled on.
I shall let it go to waste, unpruned, undug,
overgrown by brambles and thorn-bushes,
and I shall command the clouds to rain no rain on it."
Now, the vineyard of YHWH Sabaoth is the House of Israel,
and the people of Judah the plant he cherished.
He expected fair judgment, but found injustice,
uprightness, but found cries of distress.

If the mild young prophet's first utterances are a little
erudite and indirect, he soon learns to put his literary gift at
the service of a stark message, cursing the uncaring people of
Judah, "who call what is bad, good, and what is good, bad,
who substitute darkness for light and light for darkness."
Like Amos, he rails against their injustice toward the poor
and vulnerable and against their religious hypocrisy, but he
does it with unmistakable style. There are probably more
well-known quotations from Isaiah than from any other

book of the Hebrew Bible except the Psalms: "The ox knoweth his owner, and the ass his master's crib. . . . Come now, let us reason together . . . though your sins be as scarlet, they shall be as white as snow. . . . They shall beat their swords into plowshares, and their spears into pruninghooks: nation shall not lift up sword against nation, neither shall they learn war anymore. . . . What mean ye that ye beat my people to pieces and grind the faces of the poor? . . . the bread of adversity and the water of affliction."

As Amos and Hosea had threatened Israel, Isaiah threatens the dreadful Day of YHWH upon Judah, but his promise of a remnant to be saved is imbued with poetic power that they could never have matched:

The people that walked in darkness have seen a great light:
they that dwell in the land of the shadow of death, upon
    them hath the light shined. . . .
For unto us a child is born, unto us a son is given:
and the government shall be upon his shoulder:
and his name shall be called Wonderful, Counsellor, The
    mighty God,
The everlasting Father, The Prince of Peace.

And there shall come forth a rod out of the stem of Jesse,
and a Branch shall grow out of his roots:
And the spirit of YHWH shall rest upon him,
the spirit of wisdom and understanding,

the spirit of counsel and might,
the spirit of knowledge and of fear of YHWH.

But before these decidedly messianic prophecies can
come to pass, the Day of YHWH must be endured, after
which the Jews will stop relying on tyrants:

> the remnant of Israel and the survivors of the House of Yaakov
> will stop relying on the man who strikes them
> and will truly rely on YHWH,
> the Holy One of Israel.
> A remnant will return, the remnant of Yaakov,
> to the mighty God.
> Israel, though your people are like the sand of the sea,
> only a remnant of them will return.

At last, the Peaceable Kingdom shall be theirs:

> The wolf . . . shall dwell with the lamb,
> and the leopard shall lie down with the kid;
> and the calf and the young lion and the fatling together;
> and a little child shall lead them. . . .
> They shall not hurt nor destroy in all my holy mountain:
> for the earth shall be full of the knowledge of the LORD,
> as the waters cover the sea.

Though Isaiah's oracles will be preserved by his followers,
they fall on deaf ears, as had the prophecies of Amos and

Hosea. Isaiah's contemporaries are neither terrified nor thrilled by the condemnations and comforts he offers them. Though Judah has the good fortune to see two reforming monarchs—Hezekiah and Josiah—ascend the throne in a hundred-year period, it also has the misfortune to be governed by two of the worst of all the Davidic dynasty, Ahaz and Manasseh. Isaiah was an adviser to Hezekiah (715–687) and, according to legend, was sawn in two by Manasseh (687–642).

The reforming monarchs attempted to cleanse the cult of YHWH from odious Canaanite admixtures, permitting worship of the only God only in the Temple and demolishing the old sanctuaries and high places, long-tolerated venues for a syncretistic practice of Canaanite paganism and the religion of YHWH. But Ahaz and Manasseh not only tolerated the Canaanite gods but went further than any of the earlier kings of Israel and Judah (except perhaps Ahab) by offering children to Moloch, the horrible child-devouring god whose cult was practiced in the smoke-filled Valley of Hinnom* south of Jerusalem, where perpetual fires were stoked by ash-streaked priests, always ready to throw a fresh and quivering victim into the flames.

The prophet Micah, a contemporary of Isaiah's, makes reference to this charred horror when he imagines an idle devotee asking himself how best to worship God: should he sacrifice his own child so that his petition may be answered to his satisfaction?

_____

* The Valley of Hinnom is the Gehenna of the Gospels, where it is invoked as an image of hell.

"Wherewith shall I come before the LORD,
and bow myself before the high God?
shall I come before him with burnt offerings,
with calves of a year old?

"Will the LORD be pleased with thousands of rams,
or with ten thousands of rivers of oil?
shall I give my firstborn for my transgression,
the fruit of my body for the sin of my soul?"

Micah abhors such musings, which draw on this mixed tradition of Canaanite and Israelite religions but miss the point of everything:

He has already shown you what is right:
and what does the LORD require of you,
but to do justice,
love mercy,
and walk humbly with your God?

For the prophets, there is a profound link between idol worship and injustice. Baal and Astarte and Moloch are the gods of human desires: they can bestow power and riches, prestige and victory, and can be wheedled into doing so by some rigmarole or other, some offering. But our God is the God of heaven and earth, who has told us that the only acceptable offering is justice like his justice: to treat others fairly and compassionately and never to stoop to the cruelty that these quid pro quo transactions can entail—things as hideous as the sacrifice of children. The religion of YHWH has come a long way from the Binding of Yitzhak; and it is coming close to establishing a new axiom by dividing the population in two: the rich are the idolators and sacrificers of children, the poor are the righteous. But the reforms of Hezekiah and Josiah can only delay, not turn aside, the Day of YHWH, made inevitable by the chronic apostasy of the Judean remnant of the Chosen People and by the painful inequalities in their society, growing ever more acute since the days of Solomon.

In the second half of the seventh century, during the reign of Josiah, when the Books of Joshua, Judges, Samuel, and Kings were set down, there rose Jeremiah, the prophet of God's judgment, who, speaking on behalf of YHWH, might well be called the prophet of the last chance: " 'Amend your behavior and your actions and I will let you stay in this place. Do not put your faith in delusive words, such as: "This is YHWH's sanctuary, YHWH's sanctuary, YHWH's sanctuary!" But if you really amend your behavior and your actions, if you really treat one another fairly, if you do not exploit the stranger, the orphan and the widow, if you do not shed innocent blood in this place and if you do not follow other gods, to your own ruin, then I shall let you stay in this place, in the country I gave for ever to your ancestors of old.' "

In Judah it was long believed that the promises made to David concerning eternal Jerusalem and the presence of YHWH above the ark in his Temple would shield Judah— unlike the northern kingdom—from ultimate catastrophe. Jeremiah predicts the destruction of Jerusalem and its Temple and the departure of YHWH. He is very precise about what will happen: Nebuchadnezzar, the king of Babylon, which has now eclipsed Assyria in the power politics of Mesopotamia, will descend with all his forces on the people of Judah, leveling their city and Temple and reducing "the whole country to ruin and desolation." Seventy years of enslavement in Babylon will follow.

This is exactly what does happen, but not before Jeremiah is imprisoned as a traitor for speaking against the state. When he is "liberated" by Nebuchadnezzar's men after they have taken the city, they assume he is on their side and allow him to choose between exile in Babylon with the rest of the Judean upper crust or remaining behind with the scattered Judean peasants. Jeremiah chooses to remain. Jerusalem is torched, its walls leveled, its Temple pulled down, the ark lost forever, YHWH vanished. Zedekiah, the last king of Judah, is made to witness the execution of his sons, the last thing he will ever see. Following the carnage, his eyes are put out and he is taken in chains to Babylon, where he will die. Jeremiah will die in Egypt, after having been forced there by well-intentioned friends.

Nevertheless, as Jeremiah prophesied in God's words:

"Watch, I shall bring them back
from the land of the north
and gather them in from the ends of the earth."

God's people will no longer be the proud nobles of Israel and Judah but the marginalized and powerless—the blind, the lame, and the pregnant:

"With them, the blind and the lame,
women with child, women in labor,
all together: a mighty throng will return here!
In tears they will return,
in prayer I shall lead them.
I shall guide them to streams of water,
by a smooth path where they will not stumble.

"Set up your signposts,
raise yourself landmarks,
fix your mind on the road,
the way by which you went.
Come home, Virgin of Israel,
come home to these towns of yours.
How long will you hesitate,
rebellious daughter?
For YHWH is creating something new on earth:
the Woman sets out to find her Husband again."

Is this what it will take for the faithless bride to turn to her husband? Gone is the city and the Temple, gone everything that gave the Jews (for that is who they now are) their false security. Is God gone, too, or is he in this terrible exile in pagan Babylon teaching them something new—"creating something new on earth"?

By the rivers of Babylon
we sat and wept,
when we remembered Zion.

They sat by the Euphrates and Tigris, the very rivers where their story began, sat and wept and meditated on their fate. The prophets, they now knew, had told the truth, had been the spokesmen for God—and it is at this point that prophecy, which had always meant divine inspiration, comes to mean prediction: the true prophet is the one who sees the future implicit in the present; and his authenticity is confirmed when his prophecy comes true. God did not want their sacrifices, their national shrines, their outward show. He was not interested in guaranteeing their political power: he had shown them most painfully that this was of no interest to him. What on earth was this about?

To appreciate how unprepared the Jews were to pursue this line of thinking, one must take a quick look around the ancient world of the early sixth century. Religion then was about sacrifice. All peoples placated their gods in public temples, associated with kingship. The identity of god–king–priests–people was visible and unmistakable. There was no other way. If their God had destroyed their identity, what more could he possibly want from them? It was in the midst of this conundrum that the unheeded words of the prophets came back to them. God wanted something other than blood and smoke, buildings and citadels. He wanted justice, mercy, humility. He wanted what was invisible. He wanted their hearts—not the outside, but the inside.

There is no way of exaggerating how strange a thought this was. The Jews thought as did all other ancient peoples—of houses and fields, flocks and herds, gold and silver. The word which falls so easily from our lips—*spiritual*—had no ready counterpart in the ancient world. YHWH was spirit, of course, and completely unlike other gods because he was invisible and could not be represented in art. But this was precisely what had always given his people so much trouble, and they longed to depict him as other gods were depicted by their people. The closest they could come to imagining spirit was *ruach*—wind, breath—the only invisible thing that was real, real because you could see its effects. *Ruach YHWH* sometimes descended on leaders, prophets, priests, and kings, for the sake of directing the people. But the people? The people had no *ruach,* God did not descend on them.

But men and women had the breath of life, which when they died escaped their bodies as mysteriously as YHWH had abandoned his Temple. There was in every human being an "inside," which the Jews had never steadily adverted to before. Could God possibly mean that each of them was to be a king, a prophet, a priest in his own right? Was this what God had meant when he said at Sinai that he would make them "a kingdom of priests, a holy nation"? Would he make them a nation of the spirit, a nation without the trappings of a nation? It was to this "inside" realm that the prophet Ezekiel, who accompanied the people into exile, was referring when he said in God's name of the coming restoration: "I shall give them a single heart and I shall put a new spirit in them; I shall remove the heart of stone from their bodies and give them a heart of flesh." Could it be that this inside— where "the still, small voice" that spoke to Elijah resided— was the real Temple of God? The ark was lost and the Tablets of the Testimony were gone, but had not God promised through the words of Jeremiah yet a new covenant in which his Law would be written "on their hearts"? And when God told them, also through Jeremiah, to "fix your mind on the road," was he speaking of a journey of the spirit?

Those who first thought these thoughts must have felt that a great thunderclap had shaken them to their roots. They could now look back over the whole of their history— from the call of Avraham to journey into the wilderness, to the call of Moshe to lead the people from slavery to freedom, to the anointing of David, the king who sang "I," to the prophets who warned them that nothing they had yet done was enough for God—they could look back and see that God had been leading them all along, from one insight to another, and telling them a story, "something new on earth," the story of themselves.

Little is known about the Jews in their exile. The biblical authors are as loathe to describe Babylon as they were to describe Sumer and Egypt. But in the course of their sojourns in various corners of the ancient world, some Jewish refugees, relying on the trading skills they had developed during the monarchy, made new fortunes and became reluctant to leave their new homes. The period of exile, therefore, marks the beginning of the Jewish diaspora, a period that has never yet come to an end. When the Babylonians are defeated by the Persians, the Persian king Cyrus issues an edict—in 538, almost exactly seventy years after the prophecy of Jeremiah—allowing the Jews to depart. A small group return to their ancestral home, and more will follow in the years to come.

The people who return to Zion are not the people who were taken away many years before. A new generation, more cosmopolitan in outlook, coming from many of the cultural centers of the ancient world, they arrive to eke out a difficult existence in a land that had been laid waste. They also arrive with books, books that accompanied them into exile and books written while in exile. During the exile or soon after the return, the Torah reached its final form, entwining the oral literatures of Judah and Israel with the concerns of contemporary priests and scribes who, in a time that was out of joint, needed to emphasize continuity and security, which they did through the elaboration of ritual prescriptions, laws, and genealogies, adding all these to the final text.

But the lightning of the prophets and the trauma of the exile must also be absorbed. Sowing their devastated land, replanting their ruined vineyards, the people of the remnant wonder what Jeremiah meant when he said: "Look, the days are coming, YHWH declares, when I shall sow the House of Israel and the House of Judah with the seed both of people and of cattle. And as I once watched over them to uproot, to knock down, to overthrow, destroy and bring disaster, so now I shall watch over them to build and to plant, YHWH declares. In those days people will no longer say: 'The fathers have eaten unripe grapes; the children's teeth are set on edge.' But each will die for his own guilt. Everyone who eats unripe grapes will have his own teeth set on edge." The metaphor of the sour grapes: it means, of course, what it says—that each will be responsible for his own sin. No more retribution generation upon generation. The *individual* is responsible, not the tribe. As with the spiritualization of the journey and of religious obligation, the idea of the individual—the single spirit—begins to take hold, an idea that makes its way with great difficulty into this world of groups, tribes, and nations, in which all identity and validation comes only from solidarity with a larger entity.

A new literature begins to emerge. Some of it, borrowing from the literatures the Jews came to know in exile, is more like the worldly "wisdom" literature of the rest of the ancient world than like the Torah and the Prophets; and in the later books of the Bible like Proverbs and Ecclesiastes we sometimes encounter a cynicism that Gilgamesh would have been comfortable with but that would have appalled Moshe and disgusted Amos. But the cultural distance that the Jews have achieved from their own ancient literature also enables them to read it with more penetrating insight. Reflecting on the Psalms and prophecies and only now beginning to understand them, they finally pose the unasked question: why must the just man suffer? For if sin and retribution are upon the individual, what is the meaning of unmerited suffering? In the figure of Job, the good man who suffers without sin, they pose their question. But the question has no answer, only: "The LORD gives and the LORD takes away: Blessed be the Name of the LORD." They have reached that mysterious core of human life where one heart in pain speaks to another—and the other can respond in sympathy but without an answer. If there is a reason, it is a reason beyond reason.

The new literature is so threaded with such meditations that it often seems existentialist, as contemporary as today, full of the pain and joy of real existence. In the Song of Songs we meet "the Shulamite" and her lover, an unmarried couple, who play out an antiphonal game that never fails to stir the reader. She speaks first:

I was asleep but my heart stayed awake.
Listen!
my lover knocking:

"Open, my sister, my friend,
my dove, my perfect one!
My hair is wet, drenched
with the dew of night."

"But I have taken off my clothes,
how can I dress again?
I have bathed my feet,
must I dirty them?"

My love reached in for the latch
and my heart
beat wild.

I rose to open to my love,
my fingers wet with myrrh,
sweet flowing myrrh
on the doorbolt.
. . . .

His arm a golden scepter with gems of topaz,
his loins the ivory of thrones
inlaid with sapphire,
his thighs like marble pillars
on pedestals of gold.

Tall as Mount Lebanon,
a man like a cedar!

His mouth is sweet wine, he is all delight.
This is my beloved
and this is my friend,
O daughters of Jerusalem.
. . . .

"How graceful your steps in those sandals,
O nobleman's daughter.

"The gold of your thigh
shaped by a master craftsman.

"Your navel is the moon's
bright drinking cup.
May it brim with wine!

"Your belly is a mound of wheat
edged with lilies.
Your breasts are two fawns,
twins of a gazelle."

In later times rabbis and church fathers, quite undone by encountering such goings-on in Holy Writ, will explain to their flocks that the Song of Songs is an allegory—which it plainly is not. It is a celebration of a relationship, an erotic relationship, in which two people face each other repeatedly with hot admiration, even intoxication, and the reader is meant to enjoy the proceedings. As the lover advises:

"Feast, friends, and drink
till you are drunk with love!"

One wonders what Avraham would have made of this poem. And Sara, would she not have found it unthinkable that *"love is as fierce as death"* and that *"great seas cannot extinguish love"* and that a woman could be so free—and even have most of the best lines? Could any woman in history before these verses were written have asserted with credibility: *"My beloved is mine and I am his"?* Throughout the Bible there have been innumerable marriages and sexual relationships, but here for the first time is a reciprocal relationship—a relationship "face to face," with much of the mystery, drama, power, and pleasure of Israel's face-to-face relationship with God. If the Song of Songs were only an allegory, the relationship of the lovers would serve as a mere mirror for the relationship of the soul (or Israel) with God. But the Song of Songs, appearing in the Bible after the long recounting of Israel's labyrinthine relationship with God, suggests rather that this God-human relationship has at last made possible a genuine human-human relationship.

In the Book of Ruth, Job's theme of suffering and the Shulamite's theme of reciprocity are brought together in a delicately humane story, set in the generations before David. Scholars have found it impossible to date this text, some even settling for the period of the late monarchy, but many placing it in post-exilic times. This book, whatever its relation to the actual events of history, is a well-proportioned short story, just four chapters long.

We meet Naomi, a woman from Bethlehem, who during a famine migrates with her husband and two sons to Moab—Moav in our translation of Exodus, the country east of the Jordan from which Moshe viewed the Promised Land. Naomi's husband dies in Moab, and her two sons marry Moabite women. The sons also die, upon which Naomi decides to return to Bethlehem, where food is plentiful again, and she sets out with her daughters-in-law. But along the way Naomi has second thoughts: "Go back, each of you, to your mother's house," she counsels. "May YHWH show you his faithful love, as you have done to those who have died and to me. YHWH grant that you may each find happiness with a husband!" And she kisses each of them goodbye.

From the first, the reader realizes that this is a new kind of story. The main characters are all women (even the phrase "your mother's house" is startling); and they are women left in trying circumstances, not knowing where their next meal will come from. But besides this, we are presented here with a loving family, modeled on God's own "faithful love," in which people do not play power games against one another but genuinely care about each other—the daughters-in-law for their husbands and Naomi for her daughters-in-law, for though her situation is desperate, she is determined not to draw her daughters-in-law into it. On the way, she has meditated on what their plight is likely to be and resolves not to pull them down with her.

Both daughters, "weeping loudly," protest that they wish to stay with Naomi—which could only be because of their affection for her. Naomi has a tart reply: "Have I more sons in my womb to make husbands for you? . . . Even if I said, 'I still have a hope: I shall take a husband this very night and shall bear more sons,' would you be prepared to wait for them until they were grown up?" It is as if Sara the pawn had finally gotten some lines of her own, for here we hear the sharply realistic sound of ancient sisterhood, given voice at last.

After more argument, Naomi convinces one of the women to return home. But the other, Ruth, refuses, speaking the famous lines:

"Whither thou goest, I will go;
and where thou lodgest, I will lodge:
thy people shall be my people,
and thy God my God.
Where thou diest, will I die:

Yʜwʜ do so to me, and more also,
if ought but death part thee and me."

"Thee and me"—so like "my beloved is mine and I am his,"
but here in such different circumstances and yet another example of face-to-face reciprocity.

After the two bereft women reach Bethlehem, Ruth is
reduced to a gleaner, following after the reapers of Bethlehem's fields and scavenging what they have left behind
them—so that she and Naomi may eat. But she is already on
the lookout for "some man who will look on me with
favor," as she tells Naomi. The man she happens on is Boaz,
an excellent prospect, both prosperous and kind; and Ruth,
almost in the manner of a Jane Austen heroine, sets to
scheming with Naomi, who advises her on just the series of
ploys to gain Boaz's heart. All ends well, and in the course of
events, Boaz proves himself sharp, resourceful, and un-
threatened by Ruth's bold intelligence.

The story of Ruth has neither the hard-breathing ro-
mance of the Song of Songs nor the stomach-wrenching
wretchedness of Job, but it has both pain and exaltation and
the suggestion that, behind the scenes, God is at work,
bringing his purposes to fulfillment. At the story's end, following the marriage of Ruth and Boaz and the birth of a
beloved child, Obed, there is a lovely final scene of Naomi,
whose womb could bear no more sons, "taking the child,
[holding] him to her breast." In her closing comment, the
writer tells us that this beloved child will be the father of

Jesse and grandfather of David. So all suffering, however wretched, the story suggests, will have its happy outcome— sometimes far beyond the ken of any human being—and, as a peculiar Jew of the first century will write, "God works with those who love him, those who have been called in accordance with his purpose, and turns everything to their good."

Ruth and Naomi's suffering has had a purpose, which they can appreciate in their own happiness at the story's end. But only we, who can look back to the obscure beginnings of the Israelites and see their gradual transformation into a people who can understand that what is most important is invisible, only we who can see that Ruth and Naomi are an integral part of this great transformation can appreciate what has really been at stake all along:

Sometime toward the beginning of the second millennium B.C. a man named Avram was called by a mysterious Voice and told that his was to be a new destiny. He was a sharp-eyed, sharp-eared man, a wily trader and very much of his time and place, but he did something no one had ever done before him: he put faith in this Voice and upended his whole life, becoming in the process a new man with a new name and an individual destiny, a destiny that was only his, a personal vocation, not something written in the stars— something no one before him had ever imagined possible. But this destiny was also to be familial, national, and even (in some mysterious sense yet to be defined) global, for Avraham was to be the father of a great nation, a nation with a singular destiny and a unique role among the nations.

For many generations his family, now called the Israelites, passed on the story of their unique destiny, father telling son, mother telling daughter. Despite the vicissitudes of human existence that so easily wipe out group identities over time, we find this family—perhaps more than half a millennium after Avraham—in Egypt, where they have become forced labor engaged in building Pharaoh's storage cities but still aware of the old stories of their father Avraham, who talked and walked with their God. There appears among them a new leader, a tongue-tied prince, whose claims they find credible. He tells them that the God of the ancestors has spoken to him, instructing him to lead them out of their slavery and back to the land once promised to Avraham. The God has told prince Moshe his name, YHWH, and, therefore, to the ancient mind has communicated something of his essence: he is "I-will-be-there," the God of gods, the God you can count on.

Moshe has the same kind of faith that Avraham had: he believes the Voice and is willing to put his trust in it. Throughout all the ups and downs of the many years to follow—as the Israelites escape and wander, seemingly without end—Moshe remains full of hope, hope in the Promise, hope for the future—that it will be something truly new, something full of surprise. Under the surface events of this tribal story, new ideas are developing: time is becoming real; a real future is possible. And because of this, the choices I make individually are important: they make a real difference to a real future. And because all outcomes have not been predetermined in advance, the present is full of adventure and the freedom to make choices that will profoundly affect the outcome.

This great, overwhelming movement, exemplified in the stories of Avraham and Moshe, makes history real to human consciousness for the first time—with the future really dependent on what I do in the present. This movement is the movement of time, which, once past, becomes history. But the movement is not like the movement of a wheel, as all other societies had imagined; it is not cyclical, coming around again and again. Each moment, like each destiny, is unique and unrepeatable. It is a process—it is going somewhere, though no one can say where. And because its end is not yet, it is full of hope—and I am free to imagine that it will not be just process but progress.

But there are right choices and wrong choices. In order to make the right choices I must consult the law of God written in my heart. I must listen to the Voice, which speaks not only to the great leaders but to me. I must take the *I* seriously. And in this way, after many catastrophes, the people who became the Jews could begin to go from the *I* of David to the *I* of the spirit to the *I* of the individual to the *I* of compassion-for-the-*I*-of-others.

The Jews gave us a whole new vocabulary, a whole new Temple of the Spirit, an inner landscape of ideas and feelings that had never been known before. Over many centuries of trauma and suffering they came to believe in one God, the

Creator of the universe, whose meaning underlies all his creation and who enters human history to bring his purposes to pass. Because of their unique belief—monotheism—the Jews were able to give us the Great Whole, a unified universe that makes sense and that, because of its evident superiority as a worldview, completely overwhelms the warring and contradictory phenomena of polytheism. They gave us the Conscience of the West, the belief that this God who is One is not the God of outward show but the "still, small voice" of conscience, the God of compassion, the God who "will be there," the God who cares about each of his creatures, especially the human beings he created "in his own image," and that he insists we do the same.

Even the gradual universalization of Jewish ideas, hinted at in the story of Ruth the gleaner, the woman, the Moabite, the non-Jew, the classless nobody capable of friendship, was foreseen by Joel, a late prophet who probably rose after the return from Babylon:

"And it shall come to pass afterward
that I shall pour out my spirit on all humanity.
Your sons and daughters shall prophesy,
your old people shall dream dreams,
and your young people see visions.
Even on slaves, men and women,
shall I pour out my spirit. . . ."

The Jews gave us the Outside and the Inside—our outlook and our inner life. We can hardly get up in the morning or cross the street without being Jewish. We dream Jewish dreams and hope Jewish hopes. Most of our best words, in fact—*new, adventure, surprise; unique, individual, person, vocation; time, history, future; freedom, progress, spirit; faith, hope, justice*—are the gifts of the Jews.

SEVEN

From Then
till Now

*

The Jews Are Still It

It is no longer possible to believe that every word of the Bible was inspired by God. Fundamentalists still do, but they can keep up such self-delusion only by scrupulously avoiding all forms of scientific inquiry. They must also maintain a tight rein on their own senses, for, even without access to modern biblical criticism, any reader might wonder at the patchwork nature of the scriptures, their conflicting norms and judgments, outright contradictions, and bald errors. But even without resorting to modern scientific methodology or noticing what an inconsistent palimpsest the Hebrew Bible can be, we must reject certain parts of the Bible as unworthy of a God we would be willing to believe in. We read, for instance, in the Book of Joshua that God commanded the Israelites to put all Canaanites, even children, to the sword; and in the Psalms the poet regularly urges God to effect the brutal destruction of all the poet's enemies. Though the people who wrote such words may have believed they were inspired by God, we cannot.

God may be "slow to anger and quick to forgive," but he is also terrifying and at times as arbitrary (as in his dealings with Saul) as any Mesopotamian monarch. I don't think it should bother us that he is no Hallmark greeting card. If God is to be God the Creator of all, he must be utterly beyond our comprehension—and, therefore, awfully scary. More than this, I, for one, am willing to give God the benefit of the doubt in certain dubious cases—even in an episode as grotesque as the near-sacrifice of Yitzhak. He had to jump-start this new religion, and he didn't always have the best material to work with.

But it remains true that there is no way of attributing mass carnage and vindictive slaughter to a God worth believing in. Even the fiercest believer among us must, I think, admit that these operations were the work of human beings who had wrongly convinced themselves that God was on their side. The story the Hebrew Bible has to tell is the story of an evolving consciousness, a consciousness that went through many stages of development and that, like all living things, sometimes grew slowly and at other times in great spurts.

We can, however, believe that the experience on which this story is based is inspired—that the evolution of Jewish consciousness, taking place as it did over so many centuries, was animated and kept warm by the breath of God. The story of Jewish identity across the millennia against impossible odds is a unique miracle of cultural survival. Where are the Sumerians, the Babylonians, the Assyrians today? And though we recognize Egypt and Greece as still belonging to our world, the cultures and ethnic stocks of those countries have little continuity with their ancient namesakes. But however miraculous Jewish survival may be, the greater miracle is surely that the Jews developed a whole new way of experiencing reality, the only alternative to all ancient worldviews and all ancient religions. If one is ever to find the finger of God in human affairs, one must find it here.

There is nothing neat about the Bible. As the record of one "family" over the course of two millennia—millennia that are now two to four millennia distant from us—the Bible harbors all the mess and contrariness of human life. It is possible, therefore, to interpret the sprawling data contained within its covers in many different ways. We can say, with certain feminist critics, that what we have here is a collection of old husbands' tales, myths invented by a primitive patriarchy to glorify itself. But to say this we must ignore the later, personalist material, such as the Book of Ruth, and refuse to consider that the Bible is a kind of documentary record of the evolution of a sensibility, an evolution that began in the primeval worldview of Sumer. We can say that the Bible represents a revolution in which the original Earth goddess was supplanted by newly aggressive warrior males and their heavenly projections of themselves, but this hypothesis is itself a projection, a sort of feminist wish fulfillment without substantial confirmation in the archaeological record. Our best evidence suggests strongly that the aboriginal great god was always "in heaven"—that is, as completely Other as human imagination could make him—and that, because he acted on earthly life as the seed-giver, he was imagined as male.

We can force the evidence, as Joseph Campbell did, and say that all religions are cyclical, mythical, and ahistorical—and just who do the Jews think they are, pretending that their religion is based on history and therefore unique? But this sort of argument is what logicians have always called "begging the question," the logical fallacy that *assumes* as a given the very thing that must be proved. All religions *are* cyclical, mythical, and without reference to history as we have come to understand it—all religions *except* the Judeo-Christian stream in which Western consciousness took life.

We can read the Bible (as do postmodernists) as a jumble of unrelated texts, given a false and superficial unity by redactors of the exilic period and later. But this is to ignore not only the powerful emotional and spiritual effect that much of the Bible has on readers, even on readers who would rather not be so moved, but also its cumulative impact on whole societies. The Bible's great moments—the thunderous *"lekh-lekha"* spoken to Avram, the secret Name of God revealed to cowering Moshe, Miryam's song on the far shore, God's Ten Words, David's Good Shepherd, Isaiah's Holy Mountain—are hard to brush aside as merely human expressions with no relationship to the deepest meanings of our own individual lives. Nor can we imagine the great liberation movements of modern history without reference to the Bible. Without the Bible we would never have known the abolitionist movement, the prison-reform movement, the antiwar movement, the labor movement, the civil rights movement, the movements of indigenous and dispossessed peoples for their human rights, the antiapartheid movement in South Africa, the Solidarity movement in Poland, the free-speech and prodemocracy movements in such Far Eastern countries as South Korea, the Philippines, and even China. These movements of modern times have all employed the language of the Bible; and it is even impossible to understand their great heroes and heroines—people like Harriet Tubman, Sojourner Truth, Mother Jones, Mahatma Gandhi, Martin Luther King, Cesar Chavez, Helder Camara, Oscar Romero,

Rigoberta Menchú, Corazon Aquino, Nelson Mandela, Desmond Tutu, Charity Kaluki Ngilu, Harry Wu—without recourse to the Bible.

Beyond these movements, which have commonly taken the Book of Exodus as their blueprint, are other forces that have shaped our world, such as capitalism, communism, and democracy. Capitalism and communism are both bastard children of the Bible, for both are processive faiths, modeled on biblical faith and demanding of their adherents that they always hold in their hearts a belief in the future and keep before their eyes the vision of a better tomorrow, whether that tomorrow contains a larger gross domestic product or a workers' paradise. Neither ideology could have risen in the cyclical East, in Hinduism, Buddhism, Taoism, or Shinto. But because capitalism and communism are processive faiths without God, each is a form of madness—a fantasy without a guarantee. Democracy, in contrast, grows directly out of the Israelite vision of *individuals,* subjects of value because they are images of God, each with a unique and personal destiny. There is no way that it could ever have been "self-evident that all men are created equal" without the intervention of the Jews.

If it is possible to read the Bible as a hodgepodge with only a superficial unity, it is also possible to read it as a tremendous literary whole. This is the tack taken so dazzlingly by Jack Miles in *God: A Biography,* in which God is seen as a developing literary character. In quite a different way, it is also the tack taken by biblical literalists, whether Jewish or Christian, who see the Bible as a kind of "hand-

THE JEWS ARE STILL IT
249

book to life" that tells them everything they need to know. To me, at least, the most satisfying way to read the Bible is to see it as a collection of varied documents, each showing us the same revelation at different stages of development but capable of bringing us at last to a processive, personalist faith in a completely mysterious God. As Martin Buber pointed out so beautifully, it is in saying "Thou" to God that I can at last say "I" and it is in saying "I-Thou" that other "thou's" become real.

We are the undeserving recipients of this history of the Jews, this long, excessive, miraculous development of ethical monotheism without which our ideas of equality and personalism are unlikely ever to have come into being and surely would never have matured in the way that they have. This was the necessary evolution. But since it cannot be proven that God exists, it can hardly be shown that he spoke to Avraham, Moshe, or Isaiah. Each reader must decide if the Voice that spoke to the patriarchs and prophets speaks to him, too. If it does, there is no question of needing proof, any more than we require proof of anyone we believe in. For in the last analysis, one does not believe *that* God exists, as one believes that Timbuktu or the constellation Andromeda exists. One believes *in* God, as one believes *in* a friend—or one believes nothing. So, in the sense that this whole business depends on faith in God, each reader must be left to wrestle with his own, her own doubts and beliefs.

But it can be demonstrated, as I hope I have done, that the belief system we have come to call Judaism is the origin of the processive worldview, the worldview to which all

Western people subscribe, a worldview that has now taken hold in many (and, to some extent, all) non-Western societies. This "processive worldview" is regularly referred to in history, literature, philosophy, religion, and theology texts and regularly contrasted with its opposite, the "cyclical worldview," but it is seldom explained; and an otherwise well-informed humanities or social sciences student may pass through an entire degree program without ever coming to understand the meaning of these terms and their radical consequences.

In a cyclical world, there are neither beginnings nor ends. But for us, time had a beginning, whether it was the first words of God in the Book of Genesis, when "in the beginning God created heaven and earth," or the Big Bang of modern science, a concept that would not have been possible without the Jews. Time, which had a beginning, must also have an end. What will it be? In the Torah we learn that God is working his purposes in history and will *effect* its end, but in the Prophets we learn that our choices will also *affect* this end, that our inner disposition toward our fellow human beings will make an enormous difference in the way this end appears to us.

Unbelievers might wish to stop for a moment and consider how completely God—this Jewish God of justice and compassion—undergirds all our values and that it is just possible that human effort without this God is doomed to certain failure. Humanity's most extravagant dreams are articulated by the Jewish prophets. In Isaiah's vision, true faith is no longer confined to one nation, but "all the nations" stream to the House of Yhwh "that he may teach us his ways" and that we may learn to "beat [our] swords into plowshares." All who share this outrageous dream of universal brotherhood, peace, and justice, who dream the dreams and see the visions of the great prophets, must bring themselves to contemplate the possibility that without God there is no justice.

But those who claim to believe in God must contemplate a prospect no less unsettling. Throughout our Western world, though shaped by this Jewish matrix, the cry of the poor so often goes unheard. The prophets harangued Israel and Judah unceasingly about the powerless and marginalized, the overlooked widows, orphans, and "sojourners in our midst," who are still with us today as single mothers, hungry children, and helpless immigrants, wraiths invisible in our prosperous societies. Throughout the world, half of all children go to bed hungry each night and one in seven of God's children is facing starvation. Before such statistics, believers should never forget Dostoevsky's assertion that the suffering of children is the greatest proof against the existence of God; and we must ever contemplate the awful Day of Yhwh, the coming destruction of our wealth and security, the razing even of the bastions of our faith, the Temple leveled and Yhwh gone.

For without justice, there is no God.

NOTES AND SOURCES

As in the first volume in this series, I would like to give the reader not an exhaustive bibliography of everything I consulted (which, given the vastness of studies on the Bible and the ancient Near East, would dangerously increase the size of this small book) but a sense of which studies I found most valuable. The passkey to all this literature is *The Anchor Bible Dictionary* (New York, 1992), of which I was the happy publisher but for the content of which I can claim no responsibility. Its six massive volumes, ranging to every subject imaginable, make it the philosophers' stone of contemporary biblical studies. Whatever you don't know, you can learn about here. Each of the major entries gives the reader a tour of all the modern scholarship on a particular subject, as well as a guide to the many migraine-inducing scholarly controversies and, most important, a complete bibliography.

Though I cannot recommend the *ABD* too highly, it often gives the nonexpert far more than he wants, sometimes in impenetrable academese. Fortunately, a marvelous alternative is at hand—*The Oxford Companion to the Bible,* which, like all the Oxford Companions, gives the ordinary reader just what he needs to know without fuss and feathers. *The Jerome Biblical Commentary,* the work of a group of American Catholic scholars, is also highly regarded. Other excellent sources of information for the nonspecialist are the back issues of *Bible Review* and *Biblical Archaeology Review.* Both publications are edited by the legendary Hershel Shanks, who performs the daunting service of encouraging scholars of renown to write in a popular vein.

Introduction

The great modern exposition of the cyclical nature of all nonbiblical religion is to be found in Mircea Eliade's *The Myth of the Eternal Return* (Princeton, 1954; corrected second printing, 1965), but Eliade's thesis may be glimpsed under different aspects throughout his considerable *oeuvre*. Two classic works that take somewhat different tacks are James Barr, *Biblical Words for Time* (Naperville, Illinois, 1962) and Bertil Albrektson, *History and the Gods* (Lund, Sweden, 1967). The quotation from Henri-Charles Puech comes from his imposing *Man and Time* (New York and London, 1957).

I: The Temple in the Moonlight

As always when large historical movements are at issue, I find the need to consult *The Rise of the West: A History of the Human Community* by William McNeill (Chicago, 1963). The great scholarly popularizer of Sumer was Samuel Noah Kramer in *History Begins at Sumer* (New York, 1956), though I found his *The Sumerians* (Chicago, 1963) more helpful; and from this source I took all the translations used in this chapter, except for the *Gilgamesh* material, in which case I was able to use the latest and most accurate translations by Stephanie Dalley in her admirable *Myths from Mesopotamia* (Oxford, 1989). I have made one small alteration to her translation. Where she has, as the result of Enkidu's encounter with the harlot, "For Enkidu had stripped (?)," I offer "For Enkidu had become smooth"—that is, stripped of body hair—which I believe throws clearer light on this transformation and brings it closer to similar ancient tales about the transformation of a wild man or woman by means of a sexual encounter. (Compare, for instance, the ancient Irish story "The Wand of the Feat.") For the equivalent Akkadian names of all the major Sumerian gods, see N. K. Sandars, *The Epic of Gilgamesh* (London, 1972), pages 23–29. This is an attractive prose translation of the *Epic,* though considerably more coherent than the extant originals, the tablets themselves.

For readers who would like to explore further the subject of the orgy, I confess that that scene was partly of my own invention, as I imply in the text itself. I chose a male rather than a female victim because I did not wish to have the charge of male chauvinism leveled without warrant, but one early reader accused me instead of "teenage bondage fantasies," another of "homoeroticism." Since these were both friends, God only knows what reviewers may say. We know that the Sumerians employed temple prostitutes of both sexes, and we know that they conducted orgies involving priests, priestesses, and kings to attract the divine gift of fertility to themselves and their land—and we know that these rites were carried out in the context of cyclical religion. But we have no written liturgy or order of service for such events.

My description is not based entirely on imagination, however, but on an event I attended long ago in Kerry called Puck Fair. Anyone who has encountered Puck Fair will surely agree that it is the vigorous remnant of a prehistoric fertility festival. It was this experience that brought home to me the nature of the cyclical worldview (before I had read Eliade) and how far we have come from our pagan antecedents; and part of what I wished to accomplish in this chapter was to shock the reader into realizing how very different ancient cultures could be from anything in our contemporary experience. It is not the sex but the abstract and impersonal nature of the proceedings that I wish to impress on the reader. For much additional information on the sexual outlook of the Sumerians, see Jean Bottéro, *Mesopotamia: Writing, Reasoning, and the Gods* (Chicago, 1992).

As for putting moon worship in its universal context (both here and in the next chapter), my chief source was Eliade, especially his *Patterns in Comparative Religion* (London, 1958; reissued Lincoln, Nebraska, 1996). Eliade's *A History of Religious Ideas* (3 vols., Chicago, 1978) also proved helpful, as did the work of Ninian Smart, especially *The World's Religions* (Cambridge, 1989).

II: THE JOURNEY IN THE DARK

I come down heavily in favor of Avram/Avraham's Sumerian roots, a simplification which I believe does no harm. Some scholars doubt that the biblical reference to Ur is accurate and would place Avraham's beginnings among the Semites of Harran, which means "Tent City" and was a hub for caravans of semi-nomadic traders. To my mind, the most balanced presentation of the case for Avraham's Sumerian antecedents (as well as his Canaanite context) is made by William Foxwell Albright, the great figure of modern American biblical studies, in his magisterial *Yahweh and the Gods of Canaan* (London, 1968; reprinted, Winona Lake, Indiana, 1994). Though I do prefer, with Albright, to imagine Avraham as issuing from Sumer (because of the multiple traces of Sumerian thought and language throughout Genesis), my thesis is in no way dependent on Avraham's having been a Sumerian (or, more accurately, an urban Mesopotamian of Semitic origins). If he was a tent nomad or even a Canaanite (as some would press), my contention—that from Genesis onward the Bible presents us with a new way of thinking about and experiencing reality—still holds. I use the religion of Sumer not to explain Avraham but because it is the earliest religion of which we have written record. By examining it and comparing it to the archaeological "records" and later written records from all other ancient religions, we are able to see how similar they all are—and how dissimilar is Israel's religious project from all of them. This is true however we interpret the development of biblical theology. If we like, we can imagine that Avraham was a Canaanite polytheist whose beliefs were prettied up by later generations; we can even imagine that he never existed. No hypothesis (even one as radical as Jon Levenson's in *The Death and Resurrection of the Beloved Son* [New Haven, 1993], which traces the binding of Yitzhak to a Canaanite story of actual human sacrifice) can change the fact that Israelite religion, in its essential line of development, is unique among the thought systems of the ancient world and that it is responsible for the unique values of the West.

As for *when* this Israelite transformation took place, whether it began in the time of Avraham, Moshe, David, or some other figure, no one can say with absolute assurance because the texts of the Torah and the historical books of the Bible (such as Joshua, Samuel, and Kings) were reedited in later periods. In my text I (by and large) take the patriarchal stories of Genesis at face value simply because this is the clearest way of explaining my thesis. Those who would pursue further the study of Genesis should bear in mind that the mountain of theories and controversies surrounding the background of the patriarchs grows daily. For all that, E. A. Speiser's Anchor Bible volume *Genesis* (New York, 1964), from which I quote, is still the most useful general commentary. I also found helpful Nahum M. Sarna's commentary in the Jewish Publications Society's Torah series (Philadelphia, 1989) and the sprightly and insightful annotations that Everett Fox has made to his great and good translation *The Five Books of Moses* (New York, 1995). Except as noted, I use his translation exclusively throughout Chapters II, III, and IV. My only alteration to his translation has been to place direct speech in quotation marks and to substitute "[God]" for "Yнwн" in the episodes prior to the encounter at the Burning Bush, in which God first reveals his name. Most commentators assume that the use of Yнwн in earlier episodes is a retrojection of a later, more developed theology-revelation, and I saw no reason to confuse readers unnecessarily before I got to a discussion of the Name.

Indeed, throughout the text I have simplified complex questions so that the line of my argument may appear clearly. I am aware, for instance, that some consider the "world's first emperor" to have been not Hammurabi but his predecessor Sargon of Akkad. I am also aware that the Sumerian worldview had more elements of real morality than I stop to deal with. Acts of charity, in particular, were not entirely despised: like the Jews in Leviticus 19:9–10, the Sumerians were counseled not to strip their fields completely at the harvest but to leave ears of barley for gleaners—the widows and orphans who had no other sustenance. (And the goddess who protected these wretches was the same goddess who would judge mankind.) On a more exalted level, though I make no explicit reference to important modern interpretations of Genesis by such figures as Kierkegaard and Freud, the absence of their names from the text should not be taken as evidence that I am ignorant of their contributions, only that I wish to show in as uncluttered a manner as possible the development that is my main subject.

The quotations from Egyptian sources are taken from the earliest Egyptian literature: by Ptahhotpe (twenty-fourth century B.C.) and by a pharaoh (c. 2000 B.C.) whose name is lost but whose treatise on kingship is preserved in *The Teaching for Merikare,* his son and successor. These may be found in William Kelly Simpson's *The Literature of Ancient Egypt* (New Haven, 1973). For a detailed discussion of the Mayan calendar and its predecessors, see Mary Miller and Karl Taube, *An Illustrated Dictionary of the Gods and Symbols of Ancient Mexico and the Maya* (London and New York, 1993); for an interesting consideration of the cyclical element in pre-Columbian Mesoamerican society, see Dennis

Tedlock's translation of *Popol Vuh: The Mayan Book of the Dawn of Life* (New York, 1996).

The assertion that "individuality is the flip side of monotheism" came out of a discussion I had with Rabbi Burton Visotzky of the Jewish Theological Seminary of America, a man whose ordinary conversation is as studded with arresting insights as a spring garden is with daffodils.

III: EGYPT

If one may profitably spend several years reading the commentaries on Genesis, one may spend at least a lifetime doing the same for Exodus. Those who have dedicated themselves in this way should bear in mind that I am not here attempting to summarize even the major points of discussion that should occupy a class of Bible students examining this book, but only tracing the line of development in thought and emotion that runs through the Hebrew Bible and that brought into being our own sensibility. Thus I have, for instance, completely omitted the echoes in Exodus of the original Creation in Genesis and the "Second Creation" after the Flood. Israel, saved from the Egyptians and the waters of Chaos, is, in effect, God's Third Creation. But insights like this, abundant in commentaries ancient and modern, would only distract us from our main pursuit. Likewise, I barely mention the so-called monotheistic reform instituted by Akhnaton because I very much doubt that it had any effect on Mosaic monotheism—but to ford these waters would take us far afield, indeed.

I found three commentaries on Exodus particularly helpful: Brevard W. Childs, *The Book of Exodus: A Critical, Theological Commentary* (Philadelphia, 1974); Nahum M. Sarna, *Exploring Exodus: The Heritage of Biblical Israel* (New York, 1986); and Umberto Cassuto, *A Commentary on the Book of Exodus* (Jerusalem, 1967), from which I took the interpretation (by no means certain) of Rameses's name. On the philosophical infrastructure of the ancient city-state, Giorgio Buccellati's *Cities and Nations of Ancient Syria* (Rome, 1967) was illuminating.

The three lines of Miryam's Song I have taken from the King James Version but have changed its "thrown" to "flung," which I think closer to the Hebrew. Because this Song is written in a form of Hebrew that stands out as archaic within the rest of the text, I find that the King James gives us a better sense of its flavor.

IV: SINAI

My sources for this chapter are, by and large, the same as for the preceding chapter. The characterization of Jethro as a business consultant was suggested by Patricia S. Klein.

It is impossible to pinpoint exactly when each of the insights that constitute the mature Jewish religious vision first made its appearance in the minds and hearts of Israelites. For one thing, an insight often develops slowly over several generations. Concepts argued today before the Supreme Court of the United States—concepts dependent on such large ideas as democracy and civil rights—can be traced back to thinkers of the seventeenth century (and then further back, through the Christian Middle Ages to the Hebrew Bible itself!). But it can be difficult, even with a history closer to us in time, to pinpoint just when some new thought first emerged. So to say—unequivocally—that monotheism and individual destiny began with Avraham or that Moshe is responsible for new notions of time and moral behavior is more than I mean to affirm. I am, as I stated earlier, using the stories of the Bible only to make clear the line of intellectual and emotional development that made our worldview possible.

On the matter of the invention of the alphabet, I recommend a most illuminating interview by Hershel Shanks with Frank Moore Cross, "How the Alphabet Democratized Civilization" *(Bible Review,* December 1992).

V: CANAAN

In interpreting the narrative of Israel from the settlement of Canaan to the early monarchy, I found especially valuable John Bright's *A History of Israel* (3rd edition, Philadelphia, 1981), the standard and most reliable history in English, and Norman K. Gottwald's *The Hebrew Bible: A Socio-Literary Introduction* (1985), which is an excellent road map to the methods and insights, borrowed from literary studies and the social sciences, that are gradually making their way into biblical studies and replacing the older historical-critical approaches. In this regard, I should note that the newer methods have cast doubt on whether the religion of Israel was corrupted by Canaanite religion (as Samuel and Kings present the matter) or whether pure monotheism was a product, long after the Mosaic period, of an educated elite. Once again, I am not interested here in settling such matters. I take the biblical narrative at face value not because I am unaware of or in disagreement with contemporary scholarly developments but only because these newer interpretations need not overly concern us as we identify those unique values of Jewish religion that have shaped the Western world. With similar rationale, I do not deal with the current scholarly assumption that Saul's reign is presented negatively in Samuel in part because David's claim to the throne was shaky and needed legitimizing.

In this chapter and in the remainder of my text I normally use the New Jerusalem Bible (London and New York, 1985) for translations of prose passages. Because this translation occasionally employs versions of the Septuagint and other Greek manuscripts to shed light on the standard Hebrew (that is, the Masoretic) text, it will not satisfy everyone. But I find it to be of all *complete* contemporary translations the most intelligible and, where appropriate, most dignified. Where the NJB has "Yahweh," I have substituted "YHWH," to maintain consistency with the Fox translation of the earlier chapters. In one instance, I have altered the NJB text, substituting the variant reading "a portion of meat" (which I think more likely) for "a portion of dates" in 2 Samuel 6:19, the passage concerning the transfer of the ark.

To capture the power of poetic passages, I use in this chapter and, by and large, in the following ones the King James Version, because it remains of all English translations the most beautiful; but I have arranged such passages in poetic stanza form, which the KJV does not employ. I have also substituted the "YHWH" of the original Hebrew for "the LORD" of the KJV, again to keep consistency within my own text. Despite this, I have left "the LORD" in the most famous passages, such as Psalm 23, where I thought any substitution would strike the common reader as strange. Though we can be confident that David's lament over Saul and Jonathan is authentic, the other psalms I attribute to him I do with less certainty. The psalm associated historically with the transfer of the ark is not Psalm 47, which I use, but Psalm 132. In the poetic passage in which Nathan tells David the story of the poor man and the ewe lamb (2 Samuel 12:1–4), I used the NJB.

VI: BABYLON

I believe the Book of Kings is satirizing Solomon and Rehoboam and have interpreted accordingly. But nowhere could I find an adequate translation of Rehoboam's rejoinder to the northern nobles, which I have translated myself, though of course with rabbinical assistance.

For those interested in the question of how Hebrew became Hebrew, I recommend two books among the welter of possibilities: Peter T. Daniels and William Bright, *The World's Writing Systems* (Oxford, 1996), and Angel Saenz-Badillos, *A History of the Hebrew Language* (Cambridge, 1993).

Though I have not brought it out in the main text, the Sinai cave where Elijah hears the "still, small voice" should be identified with the cave in Exodus 33:21–22, where Moshe receives a major theophany—an instance of both continuity and development.

Recent scholarship has cast some doubt on how humble were Amos's origins, but I have taken the prophet at his word. For the text of his prophecies I have used the NJB, as I have for Hosea's address and for Isaiah's prophecy about the vineyard. Thereafter, for Isaiah's prophecies, as well as Micah's, I have used the KJV, substituting "YHWH" for "the LORD," except in familiar passages. For Jeremiah, I have used the NJB because of its greater accuracy.

For the Song of Songs, I have used the splendid new translation by Ariel and Chana Bloch (New York, 1995), which succeeds in rendering much of the poetry and unabashedness of the original.

There are a number of hot-button issues in biblical studies that I do not deal with here, especially the question of how accurate the biblical depiction is of Canaanite human sacrifice, of which we find no record in Canaanite literature. I have taken the Bible at its word, as much as anything because I find in other ancient societies (such as the Celts and the Maya), in which we know human sacrifice was practiced, a similar silence within their oral and written literatures. I think it only too likely that for profound psychological reasons human sacrifice was something that had to be done but could not be spoken of. But whether or not the Canaanites actually engaged in this practice or how often, my general argument is secure, even if we take the biblical descriptions as metaphor.

The "peculiar Jew of the first century" is Saul/Paul of Tarsus

(Romans 8:28). I realize that quoting at this point a man who is thought (at least in the popular mind) to have forsaken Judaism for Christianity may seem provocative; but I am not doing so as an exercise in triumphalism, still less to shore up old and (to me) painfully embarrassing arguments for supersessionism (the idea, now repudiated in most Christian theological circles, that Christianity has somehow "superseded" Judaism). I quote Paul because I could find no one else writing within the Jewish tradition who conveys so succinctly the idea I need to express at this point in my argument.

In the quotation from Joel I have used the KJV for the first line, the NJB for the remainder. The idea of the Outside and the Inside, attributed by many (see, for instance, Charles Taylor, *Sources of the Self* [Cambridge, Mass.: 1989]) to Augustine of Hippo, should most certainly be attributed to Augustine as a *conscious idea;* but there is no denying that it is present as a *phenomenon* in the Psalms.

VII: FROM THEN TILL NOW

The attitude of Joseph Campbell toward Judaism may be found throughout his work. See, for instance, *The Power of Myth* (New York, 1988). The premise of Jack Miles's *God: A Biography* (New York, 1995) that the consciousness that evolves in the Bible is God's own was first broached, I believe, by C. G. Jung in his *Answer to Job* (Princeton, 1972).

The connection between the modern philosophy (and experience) of personalism and ancient religious faith, which I touch on in this last chapter, runs deep. Two classic works, both available in many editions and translations, contain remarkable explorations of the connection: Martin Buber's *I and Thou* and Gabriel Marcel's *The Mystery of Being*. A third writer, Walter J. Ong, also sheds much light on the connection, especially in two works, *The Presence of the Word* (New York, 1967) and *The Barbarian Within* (New York, 1962). In this last work I would especially draw the reader's attention to the chapter "Voice as Summons for Belief: Literature, Faith, and the Divided Self." In this regard, I cannot resist quoting a brief sentence, found scribbled among the notes of the priest-scientist Pierre Teilhard de Chardin after his death: "A Presence is never mute."

THE BOOKS OF THE HEBREW BIBLE

The books of the Hebrew Bible are divided into three sections, Torah, Neviim, and Ketuvim, the initial letters of which form the acronym *Tanak,* the word by which the Bible is known in Jewish tradition. Here is the canon, or official list, of the Hebrew scriptures, which is universally accepted. It was established by Palestinian Jews in the early centuries of our era, though there was probably essential agreement on the list of included books by the last centuries B.C. Besides these books, there are a number of others, generally called apocryphal (by Jews and Protestants) or deuterocanonical (by Catholics and most Orthodox Christians), which lie at the margins of the canon, sometimes included, sometimes rejected. For some of these more marginal texts, we no longer possess a (complete) Hebrew version. Their appearance in some Bibles may be traced to their inclusion in manuscript copies of the Septuagint, a Greek translation of the Hebrew scriptures, made for Jews of the diaspora in the last centuries B.C.

TORAH OR TEACHING (SOMETIMES TRANSLATED LAW)
(also called the Pentateuch, that is, the Five Books)

Hebrew Title	*English Title*
Bereshit	Genesis
Shemot	Exodus
Vayyiqra	Leviticus
Bemidbar	Numbers
Devarim	Deuteronomy

The stories of the Torah are largely contained within the first two books: Genesis, covering the period from the Creation through Avraham to the death of Joseph in Egypt; and Exodus, covering the period from the Egyptian slavery of the Children of Israel through their escape under Moshe to the encounter with God in Sinai. Exodus concludes with a list of ordinances. Leviticus contains the ordinances of the priests of the tribe of Levi. Numbers is so called because it begins with a census of the desert tribes; it continues the narrative of the wanderings of the Israelites in Sinai, though interspersed with groups of supplementary ordinances, and concludes with the first Israelite settlements in Transjordan. Deuteronomy is a code of civil and religious laws, framed as a long discourse by Moshe and concluding with his death.

NEVIIM (OR PROPHETS)

FORMER PROPHETS

Hebrew Title	English Title
Yehoshua	Joshua
Shofetim	Judges
Shemuel	Samuel
Melakhim	Kings

This sequence presents the continuous story of Israel from the settlement of Canaan to the fall of Judea and the Babylonian exile. These books are histories, not "prophetic" works (as we would normally think of them), though in the course of their narratives prophets like Samuel are introduced. These books are given the name Prophets because all the great Israelite figures, starting with Moshe and Joshua, were deemed to be prophets in later nomenclature. In most English Bibles, Samuel and Kings are broken up into 1 Samuel and 2 Samuel and 1 Kings and 2 Kings.

Yeshayahu	Isaiah
Yirmeyahu	Jeremiah
Yehezqel	Ezekiel

The Twelve
(also called the Minor Prophets, because these books are brief)

Hoshea	Hosea
Yoel	Joel
Amos	Amos
Ovadya	Obadiah
Yona	Jonah
Mikha	Micah
Nahum	Nahum
Havaqquq	Habakkuk
Tzefanya	Zephaniah
Haggay	Haggai
Zekharya	Zechariah
Malakhi	Malachi

The latter prophets comprise all the books of actual prophecy from Isaiah to Malachi. The last twelve were customarily contained on one scroll.

KETUVIM (OR WRITINGS)

Tehillim	Psalms
Mishle	Proverbs
Iyyov	Job
Shir Hashirim	Song of Songs
Rut	Ruth

Ekha	Lamentations
Qohelet	Ecclesiastes
Ester	Esther
Daniyyel	Daniel
Ezra-Nehemya	Ezra-Nehemiah
Divre Hayyamim	Chronicles

The Torah is unquestionably *the* scripture of Jewish tradition, though the oft-repeated phrase "the Torah (or the Law) and the Prophets" alerts us that these two parts of scripture are viewed as virtually inseparable. But the third part of the Hebrew Bible enjoys less importance, being a diverse collection of texts not easily characterizable by any category other than "Writings." In this collection, Psalms is meant to have pride of place. The five short books from the Song of Songs to Esther, known as the Five Scrolls, are read in synagogues on feast days. Chronicles (usually broken into 1 Chronicles and 2 Chronicles in English Bibles) is a summary of Jewish salvation history, even employing word-for-word passages borrowed from Samuel and Kings. It begins with Adam; its ending, narrating the return of Babylonian Jews to the Promised Land, allows the Hebrew Bible to close with the consolation that the prophets foresaw and to offer hope to oppressed Jews of later periods.

Since the twelve minor prophets count as one scroll (or book), the Hebrew Bible contains twenty-four books, pointing up the importance in Jewish tradition of the number twelve and its multiples as signifying completeness or fulfillment. In addition to the twenty-four books, the apocryphal or deuterocanonical books, contained in the Greek Septuagint and accepted as scripture by Catholics and many Orthodox Christians, are Judith, Tobit, 1 and 2 Maccabees, Wisdom, Sira (or Ecclesiasticus), Baruch (who was Jeremiah's secretary), and the Greek additions to Daniel, namely Daniel 3:24–90 and Chapters 13 (the story of Susanna) and 14

(Bel and the Dragon). Besides these, many Orthodox Christians accept as scripture one or more of the following: 1 Esdras (in the Septuagint Ezra-Nehemiah is called 2 Esdras), 3 and 4 Maccabees, the Psalms of Solomon, and, in some cases, a few other minor works and additions. The order of books in Christian Bibles differs from the order of the Hebrew Bible.

CHRONOLOGY

This is not a complete chronology, by any means, just a reference guide to dates and eras relevant to historical episodes mentioned in the main text. All dates except those set in **bold** are approximations, in the case of dates associated with Avraham and Moshe quite debatable approximations.

3200 B.C.	Writing is invented in Sumer.
1850	*Epic of Gilgamesh* is set down. Avram/Avraham journeys to Canaan.
1750	The Code of Hammurabi is proclaimed.
1720–1552	The Semitic Hyksos rule Egypt.
1700	The Children of Israel arrive in Egypt.
1377–1358	Akhnaton rules Egypt and enforces exclusive worship of Aton, the sun god.
1347–1338	Tutankhamon rules Egypt.
1304–1290	Seti I, the likely pharaoh who "knew not Joseph" and enslaved the Children of Israel, rules Egypt.
1290–1224	Rameses II, the likely pharaoh of the Exodus, rules Egypt.
1250	The escape of the Israelites under Moshe and the encounter at Sinai.

1220–1200	Joshua and the Israelites invade Canaan.
1200–1025	The period of the Judges and the confederation of the tribes of Israel in Canaan.
1030–1010	Saul rules the Israelite confederation.
1010–970	David rules the United Kingdom of Israel.
1000	David takes Jerusalem and makes it his capital.
970–931	Solomon rules Israel. The stories of what will become the Torah begin to be collected.
966	Solomon builds the Temple in Jerusalem.
931	The United Kingdom of Israel is divided into Israel and Judah.
874–853	Ahab rules Israel with Jezebel. Elijah prophesies.
750	Amos begins to prophesy, followed, a little later, by Hosea.
740	Isaiah receives his vocation in the Temple. He begins to prophesy, followed, a little later, by Micah.
722 or 721	Israel is overrun by the forces of the Assyrian king Sargon II and its inhabitants are deported: the ten northern tribes are lost.
716–687	Hezekiah, one of Judah's last good kings, rules.
687–642	Manasseh rules Judah, establishes pagan cults in the Temple, and

	(according to later tradition) executes Isaiah.
640–609	Josiah, Judah's last good king, rules, attempts religious reform, and sponsors new editions of principal historical documents, Deuteronomy, Joshua, Judges, Samuel, and Kings.
605	Jeremiah prophesies Judah's seventy years of exile.
16 March 597	Nebuchadnezzar captures Jerusalem and begins deporting Jews to Babylon.
July–August 587 or 586	Nebuchadnezzar levels the Temple and the city of Jerusalem; fresh deportations continue for five years more.
539	Cyrus, king of the Persians, enters Babylon and gives back to the original cities sacred objects carried off to Babylon.
538	The Edict of Cyrus is proclaimed, allowing the exiles to return to the Promised Land.
Spring 537	The foundation of the Second Temple is laid.
520–515	The Second Temple is completed.
450	This is possibly the period in which Job, the Song of Songs, Ruth, and many Psalms are written.

ACKNOWLEDGMENTS

Several friends were gracious enough to read the first draft of the manuscript, including my wife, Susan Cahill, John E. Becker, Michael D. Coogan (whose polymath precision and uncommon generosity were indispensable), Neil Gillman, Herman Gollob, Jack Miles, Gary B. Ostrower, Ora Horn Prouser, Burton Visotzky, Robert J. White, and Yair Zakovitch. To them all I am most grateful, for they saved me from not a few errors and misjudgments. But I hasten to add that what errors and imbalances remain are mine alone.

Never was an editor more essential to a book than was my editor and publisher, Nan A. Talese, who sent me back to my desk to write what I only thought I had written. The people of Doubleday could not have been more supportive, and I thank especially Arlene Friedman, Jacqueline Everly, and the inventive, death-defying publicity and marketing team of Marly Rusoff and Sandee Yuen. For the beauty of this book, as of the previous one in the series, I am much in the debt of Marysarah Quinn, who designed the pages, and Kathy Kikkert, who designed the jacket. Alicia Brooks has been of incalculable assistance in many matters, especially in helping me to improve the accuracy of the text. Within Bantam, Doubleday, Dell, Jack Hoeft, William G. Barry, Katherine Trager, and Paula Breen all deserve special praise. No author could hope for a better sales force than BDD's. To them all, as to my dexterous agent, Lynn Nesbit, I am most grateful.

As I look back over the route that brought me to this study, I find I owe debts of gratitude to friends both old and new in two cities, Jerusalem and New York. In Jerusalem, I was welcomed by Rabbi Adin Steinsaltz and his assistant, Rabbi Thomas Eli Nisell, of the Israel Institute for Talmudic Publications. Their conversation served as high inspiration, as did the warm and welcoming household of Avigdor Shinan and his wife, Rachel. Dr. Shinan's gracious willingness to introduce me to his colleagues at the Hebrew University was also most helpful. Nor can I forget the generous friendship of Sami Taha. Just beyond the borders of Israel lies Sinai, where it was my good fortune to have as my guide Ahmed Yehia, who showed me many things I would otherwise have missed and enabled me to sojourn among the noble Bedouin. In New York, I was able to study the Bible at the Jewish Theological Seminary of America in an atmosphere of such beauty, friendship, and peace that its nooks and crannies will always seem like home to me. By everyone, from then provost Dr. Menahem Schmelzer through the dedicated faculty and staff to the rawest first-year rabbinical student, I was made to feel completely welcome and sumptuously comfortable. There will never be any way I can repay the intuitive help I received throughout my studies from Dr. Burton Visotzky—Burt, a man with a genius for friendship and a razor-sharp mind worthy of all his forebears. I close these acknowledgments by paying special tribute to my Hebrew class, both to my fellow students, as lively and engaged as any I have ever studied among, and to our relentless but always nurturing teacher, Dr. Zahava Flatto. To me, she is **אשת חיל**, the valiant woman whom Proverbs extols. To them all,

תודה מן הלב

INDEX OF
BIBLICAL CITATIONS

This list, which is offered as an aid to those who would explore the Bible more fully, is confined to those biblical passages quoted in the main text that contain a full sentence or more. Shorter quoted phrases can usually be located in close proximity to their longer neighbors within the biblical book under discussion. For those unfamiliar with the conventions of biblical citation: each citation begins with the title of one of the books to be found in the Bible, followed by the chapter number, followed (after the colon) by the verse number(s). An "a" indicates that only the first part of the verse has been quoted, a "b" that only the latter part of the verse has been quoted. The following citations use the chapter and verse numbering of the King James Version (which numbering is sometimes at slight variance with translations based on the Catholic Vulgate).

CHAPTER TWO

CHAPTER THREE

GENERAL INDEX

Aaron. *See* Aharon (Moshe's brother)

Abigail (wife of David), 185

Abraham. *See* Avraham (formerly Avram); Avram (later Avraham)

Absalom (son of David), 193, 198

Achilles, 34

Adam and Eve, 38, 196

"Adonai" ("the Lord"), 108

Adriel of Meholah, 182

Afterlife. *See* Immortality

Agriculture, Sumerian development of, 11–13, 16–17

Ahab (king of Israel), 210

Aharon (Moshe's brother), 111, 112, 148, 149, 157–58

Ahaz (king of Judah), 221

Ahinoam of Jezreel (wife of David), 185

Akhnaton (Egyptian pharaoh), 98–99

Akkadian (Old Babylonian) language, 6, 20, 21

Alphabet
  invention of, 150, 208
  See also Writing

Amorites, as nomads, 15–16

Amos (Judean shepherd/prophet), 211–14, 215, 216

Angels, 75

Anti-Semitism, 3–4, 152–53

Apocryphal books, of Bible, 7, 266, 269–70

Aquinas, Saint Thomas. *See* Thomas Aquinas

Architecture
  of sacred temples, 40–41
  Sumerian innovations in, 13

Ark of the Covenant, 159, 190, 191, 223–24

Art
  portrayal of Avraham and angels, 75
  reflecting cyclical worldview, 53, 63

Aruru (Sumerian goddess), 25

Asherah (Canaanite goddess), 172, 210

Assyria, conquest of Israel, 215–16

Astarte (Canaanite goddess), 172, 210

Aton the Solar Disc, 99

Augustine of Hippo, 139–40, 159, 196
  The Confessions, 199

Avraham (formerly Avram)
  character of, vs. Moshe, 162–63
  death and burial of wife, 87–88
  offers son as sacrifice, 79–84
  pregnancy of wife Sara, 73–75, 78–79
  relationship with God, 73–76, 84–87
  renamed by God, 72
  See also Avram (later Avraham)

Avram (later Avraham)
  in Egypt, 65–67, 98
  migration to Canaan, 59–60, 62–65
  migration to Harran, 57–59
  relationship with god, 69–70, 71–73

Cyclical worldview
  art reflecting, 53, 63
  concept of time in, 64, 126, 127–28,
    130–32, 145–46, 237–39
  defined, 5
  in Eastern religions, 249
  historical sense lacking in, 18–19,
    247–48
  immortality concept lacking in, 47
  processive worldview vs., 250–51
Cyrus (king of Persia), 228–29

Dalley, Stephanie, 30
Daniel (Book of), 7
David (king of Israel)
  anointed king, 188
  mythical stature of, 209
  poetry of, 177–78, 186–88, 190,
    195–97, 199–200
  Saul's hatred of, 181–86
  sense of self, 198–201
  slays Goliath, 178–81
  wives of, 182–83, 185, 190, 191–92,
    193–94
  YHWH chooses, 176–77
  YHWH's displeasure with, 194–98
Death, realm of
  in Epic of Gilgamesh, 34, 38
  in Sumerian cosmology, 41
Democracy, based on individuality, 249
Deuterocanonical/apocryphal books, of
    Bible, 7, 266, 269–70
Deuteronomy (Book of), 139, 140, 267
Dietary laws, 155
Donne, John, 112
Dostoevsky, Fyodor, 252
Dumuzi (Sumerian god), 31–32, 61–62
Dylan, Bob, 156

Earth goddess (Great Mother), 48, 247
Ecclesiastes (Book of), 7, 39, 230
Eden, 38
Education, importance to Israelites of,
    144
Egypt
  Avram in, 65–67, 98
  Joseph in, 96–98
  monotheism in, 98–99
  Moshe leads Israelites from, 117–22
  plagues on, 114, 115, 116–17
  See also Pharaohs, of Egypt
Eliade, Mircea, 40–41, 48, 55–56
Elijah the Tishbite (prophet), 210–11
Eliot, T. S., 163–64
Enki (Sumerian god), 46
Epic of Gilgamesh
  antecedents to Bible from, 34, 37–39,
    61–62
  contemporary values reflected in, 36–
    37
  death of Enkidu, 33–34
  description of Uruk, 20–21
  Enkidu as natural man, 25–27
  father in, 20, 22, 33, 37
  friendship between Gilgamesh and
    Enkidu, 27–29, 30–31
  Gilgamesh as Semitic king, 20, 22–24
  mother in, 22, 28, 37
  as myth vs. historical document, 126,
    127
  prostitutes in, 26–27, 29–30, 39
  seeking immortality, 34–36
Epic of Israel. See Bible; Torah
Esav/Esau, 88–89, 95
Esther (Book of), 7
Eternity
  ancient conception of, 126, 127–28
  See also Immortality
Eve and Adam, 38, 196
Exile, of Jews, 228–30
Exodus, story of, 113–22

Exodus (Book of)
as blueprint for modern liberation
movements, 249
dietary laws from, 155
as historical document, 125–27, 129,
153
time period covered in, 98, 267

Faith, origin of, through Hebrew God,
84–87, 93–94, 237–39
Farming, Sumerian development of, 11–
13, 16–17
Fate, origins of term, 54
Feminist theories
on Bible, 247
on the Great Mother, 48
Fertile Crescent, early communities in,
12–13, 14
Fertility
in *Epic of Gilgamesh,* 39
feared loss of, 115
moon and, 48, 53, 54
Fiedler, Leslie, *Love and Death in the
American Novel,* 29
Fox, Everett, 57, 109, 150
Future, as promise vs. predetermined,
130–32, 145–46, 237–39

Garden of Eden, 38
Gehenna, 221
Genealogies
importance to Israelites of, 57–58,
129
See also History
Genesis (Book of)
anachronisms in, 57
as historical document, 126–27, 129
Sumerian antecedents to, 38
time period covering, 267
Genocide, attempts in Egypt, 99–103

Gershom (son of Moshe)
birth of, 104
circumcision of, 111–12
Gilboa, Mount, Philistines defeat
Israelites, 186
Gilgamesh. *See Epic of Gilgamesh*
Gimbutas, Marija, 48
Ginsberg, Allen, 164
God. *See* Hebrew God; YHWH
God: A Biography (Miles), 249
Gods
of Canaan, 172, 210, 221
Sumerian patronal, 33, 60–61, 73, 84
See also specific names
Goliath, 178–81
Great Mother (Earth goddess), 48, 247
Greece, cyclical worldview, 5

Hades, 34, 38, 41
Hagar the Egyptian, 70–71, 79
Halakha, 155
Hammurabi, 58, 154
Hanging Gardens of Babylon, 12–13
Hapiru. *See* Israelites
Harran (Sumer)
Avram's migration to, 57–59
ziggurat of, 62
Ha-Shem ("the Name"), 108
Hatred, of God, 152–53
Heavens
significance to primitive man, 40–42,
48–50
See also Moon
Hebrew God
names for, 71, 89, 108–10
origin of faith through, 84–87, 93–94
patriarchs see, 71, 75–76, 89, 90, 95
See also YHWH
Hebrew language
development of, 6
pronunciation and meaning in, 108–9

saved from Sodom's destruction, 76–
77
Love and Death in the American Novel
(Fiedler), 29

Mahn-hu (manna), 133
Mamre (modern Hebron), Avram's
settlement in, 67–69
Man and Time (Puech), 5
Manasseh (king of Judah), 221
Manna, defined, 133
Mathematics, Sumerian, 16
Medicine, Sumerian, 16
Men
as prostitutes, 30, 39, 45
relationships between, valued in
warrior societies, 29, 37, 186–88
Merab (daughter of Saul), 181
Mesopotamia
early communities in, 12–13, 14
See also Babylon; Sumer
Metallurgy, 13
Metaphor
basis of all thought/language, 49–50
See also Correspondences, primitive
religious
Micah (prophet), 221–22
Michal (wife of David; daughter of
Saul), 182–83, 185, 190, 191, 192
Midwives, refusal to murder newborn
Israelites by, 99–102
Miles, Jack, *God: A Biography,* 249
Mishna, 155
Moab (Moav), 234
Moloch (Canaanite god), 221
Monotheism
combining moral and legal realms,
156–57
development of, 71–73, 84–86, 151–
52, 239–40
Egyptian pharaoh decrees, 98–99

See also Hebrew God; Yhwh
Moon
influence over primitive man, 47–48
Sumerian worship of, 39, 42–46
symbols for, 53, 54–55
Moses. *See* Moshe (Moses)
Moshe (Moses)
birth of, 102–3
character of, vs. Avraham, 162–63
circumcision of, 111–12, 130
death of, 167–69
as Egyptian name, 129
encounters Yhwh on Mount Sinai,
104–8, 110–11, 135–39, 150–51,
159, 161–62
leads Israelites from Egypt, 117–22
plagues and, 114, 115
response to broken commandments,
157–59
Myths
history vs., 126, 127, 130–31, 162–63
Sumerian, 17–18, 19, 20–39, 61–62

Nanna-Sin (Sumerian god), 42–43, 45,
54
Naomi, 234–37
Nathan (prophet), 194, 197–98, 205,
209
Nebuchadnezzar, 224
Neviim, 266, 267–68
Newman, John Henry, 148
New Testament, 7
Niebuhr, Reinhold, 169
Ninkasi (Sumerian goddess), 17
Ninkilim (Sumerian goddess), 16
Ninsun (Sumerian goddess, mother of
Gilgamesh), 22, 28, 37
Ninurta (Sumerian god), 16
Noah, 150
Sumerian antecedent to, 34, 37–38

Temple of the Moon (Ur), 39, 42–46
Ten Commandments. *See*
    Commandments
Terah, migration to Harran, 57–59
Thomas Aquinas, 109
Tiglath-pileser III, 215
Tigris-Euphrates plain, early
    communities in, 12–13, 14
Time. *See* Cyclical worldview; History
Tools, invention of agricultural, 12
Torah
    books of, 266–67, 269
    evolution of, 208, 229
    influence of environment in, 160–61
    moral prescriptions in, 153–55
    See also specific books
Tower of Babel, 62
Trade
    Sumerian, 13
    of United Kingdom of Israel, 205–6
Tribes, of Israel, 96, 189, 216
Tutankhamon (Egyptian pharaoh), 99
Tzippora (wife of Moshe), 104, 111

United Kingdom of Israel. *See* Israel,
    United Kingdom of
Ur (Sumer)
    Temple of the Moon, 39, 42–46
    Terah of, 56–58
Urbanization, development of, 11–15
Uriah the Hittite, 193, 194
Uruk (Sumer), 11
    description in *Epic of Gilgamesh*, 20–
        21
    temple of Ishtar, 21, 45
Ut-napishtim (Sumerian mythical
    figure), in *Epic of Gilgamesh*, 34–36,
        38–39, 61

Venereal disease, 16
Vocation (personal destiny), 3
    See also Individuality

Warka (Iraq), 11
Waugh, Evelyn, 77
Wheeled transport, 13
Wheel of Life. *See* Cyclical worldview
Wisdom of Solomon (Book of), 7
Women
    civilizing influence of, 29
    moon associated with, 48
    in post-exilic literature, 231–37
    symbols for, 53, 54, 55
Writing
    evolution of pictographs, 55
    invention of alphabet, 150, 208
    Sumerian invention of, 11, 16, 17–
        18, 20
    See also Symbols

YHWH
    anger at broken commandments,
        150–51, 158–59
    awakening spiritual realm, 226–28
    breath of, 177, 227
    champion of poor and powerless,
        154–55, 180, 212–14, 223, 250–52
    comforts Israelites in Sinai, 133, 134–
        35
    commandments to Israelites, 135–39
    David and, 176–77, 194–98
    Egyptian plagues, 114–17
    meaning of name, 108–10
    Moshe and, 104–8, 110–11, 135–39,
        150–51, 159, 161–62
    Saul and, 175–76, 177, 198
    self-description, 160–61, 163
    voice of, as revealed by Elijah, 211,
        227